DAYS OF THE
OLD WILD WEST

By
Carol Dean

About the Author

My name is Carol Dean and I'm married with two adult children, and five grandchildren and we all live in the North East.

I started to write children's stories to entertain my children when they were young on rainy weekends or school holidays. My son writing stories about ghosts or vampires, and my daughter drawing pretty pictures. Nothing to do with the story but very pretty.

And this is where my Granny Ridley and Charlie Dryden stories first appeared.

Charlie Dryden's crime/adventure stories have since developed into an exciting series of books for 9-15 year olds. My funny Granny Ridley series for 7-10 year olds now has a further nine books. Plus PC Polly, my commissioned work, has since made an amusing addition for 7-10 year olds to have a good giggle over.

Many other characters have appeared and entertained various age groups, (adults included) in the shape of dinosaurs, spiders, teddy bears, a panda, unicorns, a few aliens and a friendly ghost there too. My Native American series of books are proving popular with adults and young teens too and I am delighted to say that all my books are selling in many countries around the world. Literally worldwide which is brilliant.

All of which you can find out more about on my website
www.caroldeanbooks.com or follow me on Facebook.

Book cover: Image by Charles Marion Russell - adapted from his painting "Smoke of a .45"
Bullet Holes: Image by Calmer-Free-Vector-Images from Pixabay

ISBN 979-8-80776-198-9

Also By Carol Dean

NATIVE AMERICAN SERIES

Comanche Life
A Man Called Sitting Bull
Geronimo and Cochise – Two Apache Legends
The Trail of Tears
Quanah Parker One Man Two Worlds
They Too Played Their Part
Where Everyone Knows Her Name
The Footsteps They Left Behind

THE WILD WEST

Days of the Old Wild West

CHARLIE DRYDEN SERIES

Charlie Dryden's Cricket Ball
Help Me Charlie Dryden
Charlie Dryden Finds a Bone
Charlie Dryden and the Charnwood Abbey Ghost
Charlie Dryden and the Guardian
Beware Charlie Dryden
Charlie Dryden and the Stolen Roman Standard

DINOSAUR STORIES

Spotty the Dinosaur
Terry Comes Out of His Shell
Spike Gets a New Sister
Deano and the Baby Dinosaur

Deano Has Lost His Roar
Reggie Learns a Lesson
Herbie's Big Day

STORIES FOR EVERYBODY

Sophie the Suffragette
Webster Swings into Action
The Day the Ghost Got Scared
Amelia Flurry and the Legend of the Unicorn
Mr Mortimer Meets the Aliens

PC POLLY

PC Polly the Police Lady
Be Safe Be Seen PC Polly

PC Polly on Patrol
PC Polly and the Mini Police

CHRISTMAS STORIES

Santa Steams Ahead
Santa and the Magic Dust
The Day Santa Met Santa

GRANNY RIDLEY SERIES

Granny Ridley Tries Exercise
Granny Ridley Knows the Way
Granny Ridley Goes on a Trip
Granny Ridley in the Snow
Granny Ridley and the Alien

Granny Ridley Helps Out
Granny Ridley Tries Knitting
Granny Ridley Has a Weekend Away
Granny Ridley and Wolfie
Granny Ridley Gets the Runs

YOUNG READERS

Peter the Panda is Hungry

Teddy Has Lost His Growl

WAR STORIES

Ponsonby-Smallpiece - The Legend

You can find all Carol's books on her website www.caroldeanbooks.com.

CONTENTS

FOREWORD

For those of you who have read any of my Native American series of books, you will understand that my interest in 'Cowboys and Indians' started at a very early age, with a gift of a historical encyclopaedia on this subject from my lovely Grandad. It told me the true story and I soaked it all up even at that early age and this subject has been my interest and inspiration ever since.

Admittedly, this was a long time ago now, but that interest has never left me. Sadly the encyclopaedia left me rather suddenly when I was nine years old and its disappearance was totally out of my very young control. And I have spent years searching second hand book shops, jumble sales etc. in the hope that one day I will find and replace my favourite book. As yet, sadly, I haven't.

Despite this I am pleased to say that I have achieved my goal of writing a series of Native American books featuring some of my heroes and the trials, tribulations and despair they faced just trying to live. Not exactly a laugh a minute, but it happened and the repercussions are still being felt.

This book concentrates on the Wild West from the perspective of the early Americans. Looking into the early days when the West was in its discovery days leading up to the reputation it had of being 'wild' and beyond.

And it also brings in some of those pioneers of the Wild West, including some of the more famous names, who earned their reputation from the barrel of a gun. Some dying that way too, as there was always someone willing to try their luck at being a faster draw with the gun. Get into a fight, shoot someone in the street and no one cared. Life was cheap. If you were in town and you owned a gun you were deadly. If you were out on the plains without a gun you were dead. Simple as that.

This was the land of opportunity and many headed there to start new lives. The original inhabitants being gradually squeezed off their land and then squeezed into very small reservations.

But this new land opened up a new world for immigrants and settlers from all areas, England included. With them came the card sharps, the trappers, the buffalo hunters, the cowboys and the outlaws. All in all it was a dangerous place to be, but that didn't stop the settlers coming too.

But by writing about the Wild West, this gives me the opportunity to dedicate this book to those 'Legends of the West' that I am sure you will have heard of, now immortalised in many a film and book. Mine included.

Usually at the end of my forewords in each of my books, I say *'Enjoy'*. But this time something else seems more appropriate.

'YEE HAH'

Carol Dean

TIMELINE

I have also picked just a few of the dates from the list *(in bold Italics – please see end of timeline)* to show you what we in England were achieving on those particular timelines.

1804: 17th March - Trapper Jim Bridger was born

1840: Texas Rangers were formed into a special division of soldiers with the sole purpose of fighting the Comanche on the Comancheria

1887: 8th November - Doc Holliday died

1908: 7th November - Butch Cassidy and the Sundance killed in a shootout in Bolivia (possibly)

1804: 10th May – William Pitt the Younger begins his second premiership as Prime Minister

1840: 10th January – Uniform Penny Post introduced, replacing the Uniform Fourpenny Post of 1839

1887: Buffalo Bill's Wild West tours Europe

1908: 24th January – start of publication of Robert Baden-Powell's Scouting for Boys in London

AMERICAN WESTWARD EXPANSION

1810-1890

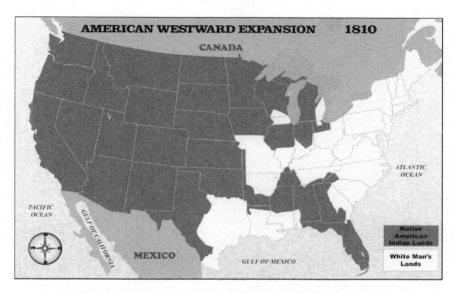

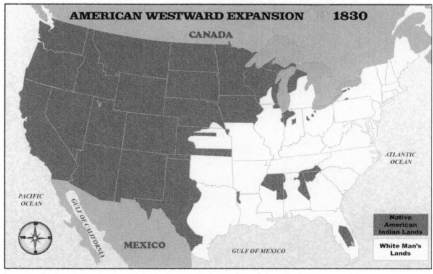

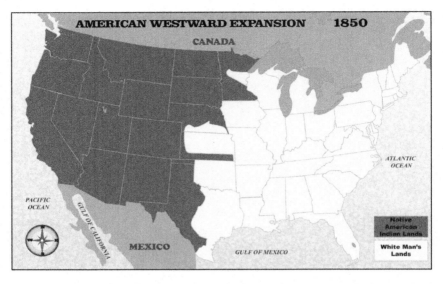

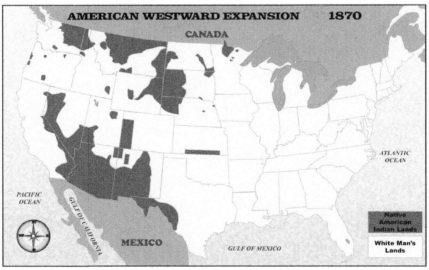

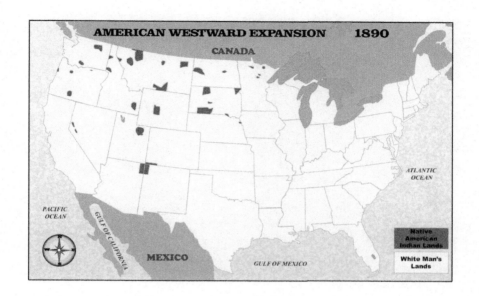

THE WAY WEST

Public Domain Image

LOUISIANA PURCHASE

William Morris (https://commons.wikimedia.org/wiki/File:Louisiana_Purchase.jpg)
https://creativecommons.org/licenses/by-sa/4.0/legalcode

        The year is 1803 and Napoleonic France had just agreed to sell land from the Mississippi River in the east to the Rocky Mountains in the west, and from the Gulf of Mexico in the south to what is now Canada in the north, to the United States for fifteen million dollars.

'The purchase of this land included two Canadian provinces, including the entirety of Arkansas, Missouri, Iowa, Oklahoma, Kansas, and Nebraska; large portions of North Dakota and South Dakota; the area of Montana, Wyoming, and Colorado east of the Continental Divide; the portion of Minnesota west of the Mississippi River; the north eastern section of New Mexico; northern portions of Texas; New Orleans and the portions of the present state of Louisiana west of the Mississippi River; and small portions of land within Alberta and Saskatchewan. At the time of the purchase, the territory of Louisiana's non-native population was around 60,000 inhabitants, of whom half were African slaves.' Wikipedia

The Louisiana territory had been controlled by France from 1699 until it was ceded to Spain in 1762.

In 1800, Napoleon was the First Consul of the French Republic, and had regained ownership of Louisiana as part of his huge plan to re-establish a French colonial empire in North America. However, France failed to stop a revolt in the area of Saint-Domingue, and the possibility of another war with the United Kingdom, prompted Napoleon to consider selling Louisiana to the United States.

Acquisition of Louisiana had been a long-term goal of President Thomas Jefferson, as he wished to be in control of the crucial Mississippi River port of New Orleans. Trading was important.

Jefferson tasked James Monroe and Robert R. Livingston with purchasing New Orleans. Their task was to negotiate with French Treasury Minister François Barbé-Marbois (who was acting on behalf of Napoleon). The American representatives quickly agreed to purchase the entire territory of Louisiana after it was offered. Funding was found for the new acquisition called the Louisiana Purchase.

France had only controlled a small portion of this area, most of it was inhabited by Native Americans. What the United States bought **'was the "preemptive" right to obtain "Indian" lands by treaty or by conquest, to the exclusion of other colonial powers'**.

The United States was now twice its size. But as these lands were already inhabited by Native Americans help was needed to find out where they were.

Information was needed to locate where they lived and what resources abounded on this new acquisition. Jefferson needed men who he could trust to explore and conquer these unknown lands, set up trading and open up the land for expansion.

Jefferson chose Captain Meriwether Lewis for this vast task and in turn Lewis chose William Clark to assist him. The Lewis and Clark Expedition spanned from 31st August, 1803 to 25th September, 1806, and was also known as the Corps of Discovery Expedition.

Their task was to explore and map the newly acquired territory, find a useable route across the western half of the continent, and to establish an American presence in this territory before European powers tried to lay any claims in the area. They were also tasked with 'scientific and economic studies of the area's plants, animal life, geography and to establish trade with local Native American tribes'. When the expedition was over Jefferson wanted to see detailed reports on its findings with maps, sketches, and journals comprehensively written and researched. Quite a task.

Public Domain Image

"The object of your mission is to explore the Missouri River, & such principle stream of it, as, by its course and communication with the waters of the Pacific Ocean, whether the Columbia, Oregon, Colorado or any other river may offer the most direct & practicable water communication across this continent for the purpose of commerce."

With their newly minted Indian Peace Medals with a portrait of Jefferson and inscribed with a message of peace and friendship, the Corps of Discovery headed off on their mission.

During their journey, Lewis and Clark encountered many differing tribes, who themselves, were quite used to Americans due to the trading they already had in the Mississippi area.

Further afield, they came into the unchartered territory on the prairie lands in what we know as Nebraska today. Many of the tribes they encountered seemed to be friendly enough, although 'conversation' was attempted through a form of sign language. Difficult at first but they achieved what they needed to know.

The Lakota, on the other hand, were none too keen on having these interlopers arriving on their land and passing through their hunting grounds scaring the buffalo. So Lewis and Clark moved on.

With the help of Shoshone female Sacagawea, the 16 year old wife of a French Canadian fur trapper Toussant Charboneau, they were able to establish good contacts with local Native Americans, set up trade, and show the hand of friendship through her knowledge of various languages. Without Sacagawea's help this may not have been such an easy expedition for them. What Sacagawea didn't realise was the help she was giving Lewis and Clark would lead to the eventual removal of her people and other Native American nations from the land.

On their journey Lewis and Clark began to understand the 'lay of the land' and managed to map out the area quite accurately. They produced about 140 maps documenting any natural resources and many plants that had not been seen by the American eye, but used by the Native Americans they encountered.

Lewis and Clark were the first Americans to see Yellowstone, and produced an official description of these different regions. Their visit to the Pacific Northwest, the maps they produced, and the many 'proclamations of sovereignty' with medals and flags were the start of the legal steps needed to claim title to each Native American nation's lands under the Doctrine of Discovery. **'The Doctrine of Discovery established a spiritual, political, and legal justification for colonization and seizure of land not inhabited by Christians.'** Wikipedia

Jefferson was keen to know the location of the Native Americans, their strength and numbers, how they lived their lives, their cultures and activities. These reports were of great interest to him. The expedition located around 200 new plants and an abundance of animal species too. It looked like a good place to be.

But the expedition was also to make sure that the Native Americans understood that their lands now belonged to the United States and that *'their great father'* in Washington was now their sovereign.

And it seemed that no sooner had Lewis and Clark finished their expedition and returned home as heroes, that the trappers started to move in, following Lewis and Clark's path on this new found land.

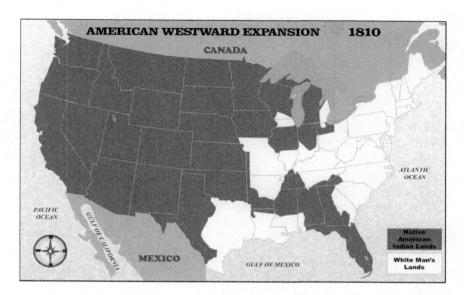

JIM BRIDGER

Public Domain Image

Trappers such as James Felix Bridger, or Jim Bridger as he became known, was a pathfinder once Lewis and Clark had explored the area.

Born on 1804 it was not long before this trapper, explorer, hunter, scout and guide headed out into this new world.

He and many others, known as 'mountain men' were made of very hardy stuff and paved the way for settlers to move into this new land.

Bridger was not only a pathfinder, as he became well known for participating in numerous expeditions mediating between Native American tribes and enthusiastic settlers. A form of trust was there between himself and the Native Americans.

But Bridger was inspired to become a trapper when in the early 1820s a General William Ashley, of the Missouri militia, and his long-time friend Major Andrew Henry, came up with a new money making scheme in the fur trade.

They targeted the local St. Louis area in 1822, and they published an ad placed by the Ashley-Henry Trading Company, in the *St. Louis Enquirer*. They wanted ***"One Hundred enterprising young men to ascend the river Missouri to its source, there to be employed for one, two, or three years."*** Bridger was now 22 years old and keen to be part of this.

The men they were looking for became more than "mountain men". The skills needed for the role were simple, you had to be masculine, well-armed, and able to use your firearm well, as well as work (trap) for up to three years. They had to get used to the hardships and extreme conditions of the Rocky Mountains from southern Colorado to the Canadian border. And, more importantly, be able to work and survive in those conditions working to keep the now popular fur trade with plenty of supplies.

The use of a gun was an essential item out there in the wilds. And you were taught from a very young age, as a matter of necessity, to use a rifle, or a knife not only to protect yourself, but also your family too. It was all part of survival. Shoot to kill whether it was to save your life from a threat, or to save your life through the killing of the animals you needed for food, again to survive out there. Many legends started their shooting skills from very early ages and some had become lethal with the gun and were feared for it for years.

But the skill that was needed in this instance was for survival and progress, and the ad attracted many willing men as around 180 signed up. Among those hired was Jim Bridger, and he became well known as a frontiersman. Although unable to read or write, he was to become a linguist speaking French, Spanish and quite a few Native American languages too.

al guy contribs
https://commons.wikimedia.org/wiki/File:RockyMountainsLocatorMap.png
RockyMountainsLocatorMap
https://creativecommons.org/licenses/by-sa/3.0/legalcode

These new hard working trappers and hunters moved ahead of settlers, searching out new supplies of beaver and other skins for shipment to Europe. The hunters were the first Europeans in much of the Old West and they formed the first working relationships with the Native Americans in the West.

Bridger's exploring in 1824, led him to be one of the first mountain men to see the natural wonders of Yellowstone springs and geysers. They are amazing. I know this as I have been there, but it must have been something wondrous to behold particularly being one of the first to actually see them.

anonymous
https://commons.wikimedia.org/wiki/File:Yellowstone_Grand_Geysir_02.jpg
Yellowstone Grand Geysir 02
https://creativecommons.org/licenses/by-sa/3.0/legalcode

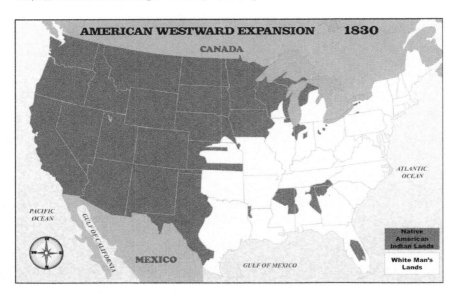

In 1830, Jim Bridger and several of his friends, decided to take over the Rocky Mountain Fur Company for profit making purposes. But competition for fur was great and this motivated many of the trappers to explore much deeper into the land itself.

This worked out well not only for the much sought after fur, but it gave a further understanding of the land and its animal resources. But that sought after fur led to the vast depletion of the beaver population. A good beaver skin could bring in as much as $4 for one which was huge when the average wage per day for a man could be as little as $1 per day.

Trapping always took place in the fall when the fur was at its prime and once the summer had arrived then it was time to meet up somewhere near the Green River area of Wyoming, to sell their furs, renew supplies for the next winters trapping, and 'whoop it up' a little while they were there. And 'whoop it up' they did, dancing, singing, telling tall tales of their adventures, and frolic too.

This, and a change in the style of fur hats, eventually finished the Rocky Mountain Fur Company. A once healthy population of beaver, otter, bear and muskrat disappeared and it became harder and harder to catch anything in a trap. The trade in beaver fur virtually ceased by 1845.

By 1834, not really enjoying being a business man, Bridger sought the only option and that was to sell out to a new firm, The American Fur Company. Bridger married a Flat Head woman called Cora, and although they worked together still trapping, this life seemed to have lost its edge for Bridger. He had other ideas.

It was during this time that Bridger and a man called Louis Vasquez established a fort, Fort Bridger, on the Green River part of the Oregon Trail. Bridger felt that there was enough passing trade with the new settlers pouring into the area that a trading post would be successful. Fort Bridger helped with trade, as supplies would be brought in and it turned out to be a good stopping point to gain extra supplies.

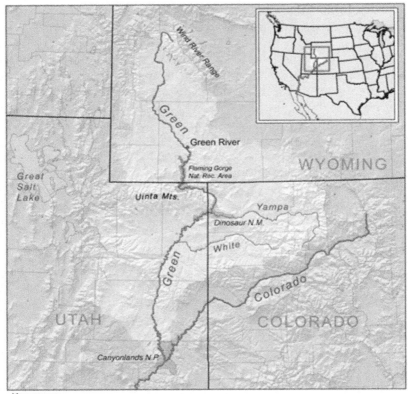

Kmusser
https://commons.wikimedia.org/wiki/File:Greenutrivermap.png
Greenutrivermap
https://creativecommons.org/licenses/by-sa/3.0/legalcode

By 1850, Bridger had fallen upon a route which was then called the Bridger Pass which shortened the Oregon Trail by 61 miles. The Bridger Pass became the chosen route of the Pony Express, the Overland Stage, and the Union Pacific Railroad.

Bridger continued his role as guide as he had the knowledge and experience of working and staying alive in these wild areas. He used his skills to advise wagon trains on their best routes.

Fort Bridger was sold in 1858 and Bridger then served as a scout for Colonel Henry B. Carrington during Red Cloud's War (1866-1868) and was also at Fort Phil Kearny during the Fetterman Massacre (a battle during Red Cloud's War between the Lakota, Cheyenne and Arapaho and the US Army based at Fort Phil Kearny). The fort was there to protect travellers on the Bozeman Trail.

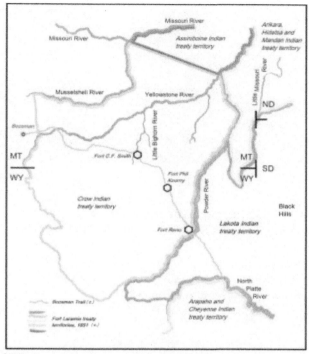

Naawada2016
https://commons.wikimedia.org/wiki/File:Bozeman_Trail,_the_forts_and_
the_Indian_territories.jpg
https://creativecommons.org/licenses/by-sa/4.0/legalcode

Ten warriors, including Crazy Horse, lured an unsuspecting Captain William J. Fetterman and his 81 men into an ambush. All were killed and this was named the *'worst military disaster ever suffered by the US Army on the Great Plains'.*

Bridger was also at the Wagon Box Fight where in 1867, again during Red Cloud's War and near Fort Phil Kearny, where 26 US Army soldiers and civilians were attacked by several hundred Lakota Sioux. Sadly the Lakota Sioux numbers did not help them against the army's Springfield Model 1866 rifles and the lever action Henry rifles. Plus the US Army used the wagon boxes as protection during the fight hence the name. The attack lasted for hours but casualties were very low. But the US Army did lose horses and mules to the Lakota Sioux, so in effect both sides won.

Public Domain Image

It was not long after this that Bridger was discharged from his role as scout as in 1868 as he was suffering from a goitre and rheumatism. By 1875 he was sadly blind. He died on his farm in Kansas on 17th July, 1881, at the age of 77 years.

He will be remembered as 'one of the most colourful and widely travelled mountain men of his era, and well known for his storytelling.'

Hunakai MJ Clark, artwork by David Alan Clark
https://commons.wikimedia.org/wiki/File:JimBridgerDetail.jpg
JimBridgerDetail
https://creativecommons.org/licenses/by-sa/3.0/legalcode

KIT CARSON

Another famous mountain man was Kit Carson. Carson began at the age of 19, when he travelled through many parts of the American West with famous mountain men like Jim Bridger.

Public Domain Image

Public Domain Image

Carson was a fur trapper, wilderness guide, Indian agent, and US Army officer. In the Apache Wars, Colonel Christopher "Kit" Carson forced the Mescalero Apache onto a reservation in 1862. In 1863–1864, Carson used a 'scorched earth' policy in the Navajo Campaign, burning Navajo fields and homes, and capturing or killing their livestock. He was helped by other Native American tribes who had no love for the Navajos. The Navajo were forced to surrender.

Carson also became a frontier legend in his own lifetime through biographies, news articles, and exaggerated versions of his exploits were the subject of many dime novels making Carson a legend.

'His understated nature belied confirmed reports of his fearlessness, combat skills, tenacity, and profound effect on the westward expansion of the United States. Although he was famous for much of his life, historians in later years have written that Kit Carson did not like, want, or even fully understand the celebrity that he experienced during his life.' Wikipedia

Kit Carson died on the 23rd of May, 1868 aged 58.

OREGON TRAIL – SANTA FE TRAIL

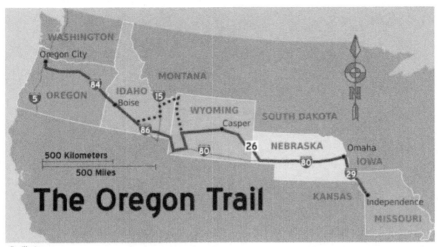

The Oregon Trail was 2,170 miles long and was an east/west route for wagon trains bringing new settlers keen to head to the valleys of Oregon. It started in Independence, Missouri, and ended in Oregon City travelling through six different states. This land was free for the taking. It was fertile and appeared to have a disease free climate. The land was perfect.

The trail itself was originally laid by the fur trappers from about 1811 to 1840 and was originally only passable by horse or on foot. Various trappers discovered the land during their fur trapping mountain men days, and some were able to report back on the resources and variety of animal species as some were able to produce diaries of their travels. This allowed them to become guides to the wagon trains as the trail became used more and more by settlers. Bridger used his knowledge and skills living in this area and would often give guidance to the wagon trains heading out.

Each improvement to the trail including bridges, ferries and roads, added to the availability of the trail for travellers making the Oregon Trail quicker and safer, as it could take up to five months from end to end.

From about the mid-1830s, the trail was used by about 400,000 settlers, miners, ranchers and business men and families. Very determined people looking for a new life. In 1978 about 300 miles of the trail that is still remaining was preserved and named the Oregon National Historic Trail.

When the settlers started arriving from east to the west, although the Native American was already living there at the time, the settlers saw the land as "empty".

During 1821 another route called the Santa Fe Trail was used extensively by settlers and trappers alike. The route itself had been used prior to this by Native Americans as well as early trappers as a route to trade after the Louisiana Purchase.

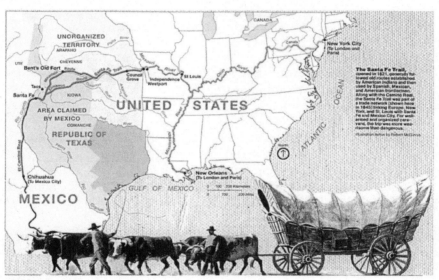

Public Domain Image

But this trail crossed the north western edge of the Comancheria, territory belonging to the Comanche. This caused much disruption due to the Comanche trying to gain their land back. But the increased traffic of wagon trains 'hell bent' on gaining this wonderful free land disrupted the migration of the buffalo herds too, as they were unable to then graze where they had done for centuries, as the settler had moved in and stayed. This began the demise of the Comanche too as their way of life was jeopardised, and their main source of food and clothing was now at risk.

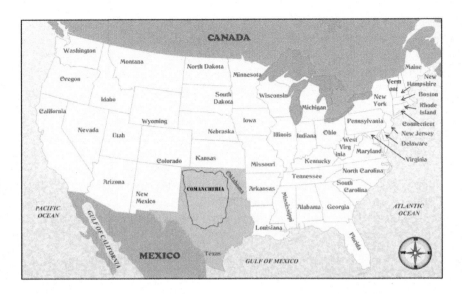

This was all part and parcel of the US Government's Manifest Destiny. *'The 19th-century doctrine or belief that the expansion of the United States throughout the American continents was both justified and inevitable.'* Wikipedia

The Santa Fe Trail was vital to the transportation of products from the central plains of St. Joseph and Independence, Missouri, connecting it to port cities along the Mississippi and the wagon train outfitters. From 1822 the US Government increased its efforts to really open up the Santa Fe Trail and increased trade with Mexico to get more settlers in.

But it wasn't an easy journey and could not be taken on lightly. Travellers in wagon trains faced huge hardships with a challenging hundreds of miles to be endured as well as the terrain of hot deserts and the steep Rocky Mountains. But also the weather brought very, very hot dry days during the summer months. This intense hot weather dried up any chances of fresh water on the trail too. Plus the freezing temperatures during the winters that seemed never ending. There were very few places you could gain shelter either from the heat or the cold and often travellers would lose their stock as they got 'spooked' during a very heavy and sudden thunder storms.

If lack of water or shelter wasn't enough, add to this the very definite chance that you could be bitten by a snake, or stung by a scorpion, or attacked by unhappy Comanche or Apache. It was a chance you had to take if you wanted to travel in those days.

But none of these hardships really deterred the settlers heading into this glorious land of opportunity. Travellers that also included gold miners, fortune seekers, and buffalo hunters.

Because of this and the hardships they faced, you cannot help but admire their determination and bravery in wanting to be part of this unknown new world.

Many had used the last of their funds just to get

Public Domain Image

equipped for the journey. This meant that if, in order to continue to your destination, you had a river to cross or navigate then you may not have had the funds to pay passage.

Did they give up? Not a chance. Trees would be felled, chopped and made into a makeshift raft. With their worldly goods precariously balanced, the journey into the unknown would continue.

And travelling with them, unseen, was something even worse. DISEASE.

The enthusiastic settlers were an unhygienic lot. But then again what hygiene could you have on the trail? But the lack of hygiene and the conditions they lived in while travelling had an impact on them all.

Diseases that spread so quickly that travellers didn't stand a chance. They had nowhere to go to keep themselves and their families safe. Diseases like this had never been seen before.

Smallpox was spread through the land as the settlers travelled through it. Cholera killed so very fast, that once you were infected it could kill a healthy adult in a few hours. And it was a terrible way to die with all the horrific effects as the disease took hold. Many hopeful settlers never got anywhere near their dream coming true. Some tried to save themselves and their families by leaving an infected wagon train to join another thinking they were getting away from the disease at last. But they only infected more people on the other wagon train and more died sadly.

Water supplies were quickly contaminated, and as cholera gave you a terrible thirst. Drinking from the barrel of water only spread the disease quicker to others, unbeknown at the time, and that only made matters worse. The disease was passed on so quickly. Diarrhoea, vomiting, dehydration, desperate thirst, aching limbs, kidney failure followed by death.

It's unknown how many settlers were left buried on the trail, from disease, exhaustion, or accidents on the trail. They would literally be buried right in the middle of the wagon train path so that the wagons and animals trampled over any signs of a burial and no scents could be located by roaming wild animals as the bodies were buried very deep. They had to be. The only consolation for the grieving families would be that wolves, coyotes or cougars could not pick up the scent of death and dig up the bodies.

Public Domain Image

But none of these horrendous hardships stopped the flow of wagon trains with their sizes increasing. The land was 'the promised land' to the settlers and to try and deflect attacks from Native Americans, they increased the numbers of wagons. Safety in numbers perhaps? But they did learn the hard way that the Comanche would not raid a wagon train to steal their oxen or mules. They wanted horses. So the settlers took more oxen and mules.

On 9th February, 1880 the Santa Fe Railway Company railway arrived and ended the need for the Santa Fe Trail. Everything became easier by rail.

SHAPING THE WEST

Public Domain Image

SHAPING THE WEST

Now things were beginning to change and a lot seems to have happened from now on. It changed the shape of the West and it's really a time when the West started to become 'wild'.

Some of the names you might recognise were born into this era such as, William Frederick Cody (Buffalo Bill Cody), Wyatt Berry Stapp Earp, Alexander Franklin James, Jesse Woodson James, Patrick Floyd Jarvis Garrett, John Wesley Hardin and John Henry Holliday. And it wasn't long before they appeared as major players in the Wild West.

It may have seemed like a lawless time, but there were these fearless men who stood their ground and were not afraid to shoot first and ask questions later. Some of those men were Texas Rangers.

TEXAS RANGERS

The Texas Rangers were a group of young men employed by the founder Stephen F. Austin in 1823. He was known as the 'Father of Texas' and it is said that he employed ten men to act as rangers to protect 600 to 700 newly settled families who arrived in Mexican Texas following the Mexican War of Independence. They were first led by a Captain Morris.

The Texas Rangers' role was officially started in 1835, and the first Major of the Texas Rangers was a man called Robert McAlpin Williamson. Within two years the Rangers had grown to consist of more than 300 men.

The Texas Rangers were also known as "*Los Diablos Tejanos*" — "the Texan Devils" because they were so 'ruthless and lethal' against the Mexican guerrillas, that people feared them.

Public Domain Image

The Texas Rangers had made history themselves by being part of major events in Texas and being involved in some of the more famous criminal cases such as, gunfighter John Wesley Hardin, bank robber Sam Bass, and outlaws Bonnie and Clyde in the 1930s.

In the 1840s, the Texas Rangers were formed into a special division of soldiers with the sole purpose of fighting the Comanche on the Comancheria, and making sure that the Comanche stayed away from the settlers.

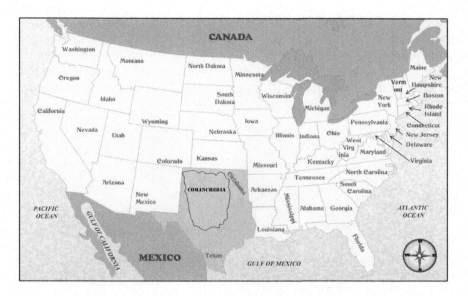

This added protection brought many more settlers and gold miners to the Comancheria which gave the Comanche much distress as they brought with them disease, and they frightened off the buffalo herds, their only main food source.

The US Army had limited forces to protect any settlers at all and a task force such as the Texas Rangers was an enormous help to them.

Pursuing the Comanche and other tribes, just to protect the settlers which also would ultimately lead to the moving of the Comanche tribe away from the land, was their main orders. And the Texas Rangers continued to carry out their orders.

Texas Rangers as a whole didn't have a particularly good reputation as they were said to be *'a violent undisciplined bunch of young men in their 20s, wearing whatever they could find.'* Although paid sometimes, they were classed as volunteers with the main aim of killing

Comanche. But they were superbly mounted, "armed to the teeth" with a large assortment of weapons, and obviously at home on the land.

The Texas Rangers continued to battle with Native Americans through 1846, and played important roles sometimes acting as guides and using - guerrilla warfare tactics, which soon established them with a fearsome reputation among both Mexicans and Americans.

They played and huge role in the defeat of the Comanche, Kiowa and Apache people. The Apache *"dreaded the Texas Rangers...whose guns were always loaded and whose aim was unerring; they slept in the saddle and ate while they rode, or done without...when they took up our trail they followed it determinedly and doggedly day and night."*

Public Domain Image

TRAIL OF TEARS

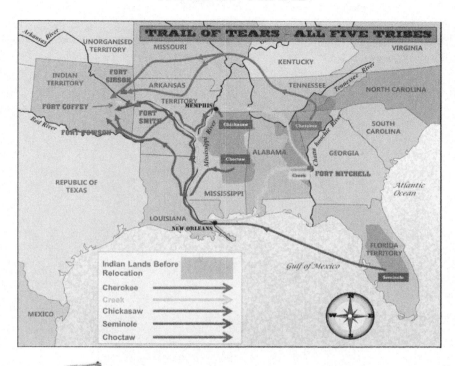

1830 brought about a huge push from the US Government to remove Native Americans from their homes. This came about when President Andrew Jackson, who was an ambitious man, became the 7th President of the United States in 1829.

It was during his presidency that the idea of removing the 'Indian' from their lands became a reality when in 1830 he signed the Indian Removal Act, which gave the federal government the power to *'exchange Native-held land in the cotton kingdom east of the Mississippi for land to the west, in the "Indian colonization zone" '*, classed as part of the Louisiana Purchase. (This "Indian territory" was located in present-day Oklahoma).

The Five Civilised Tribes involved were Cherokee, Creek, Chickasaw, Seminole and Choctaw. The removal was called 'The Trail of Tears' by those Native Americans involved whereas the US Government called it 'The Indian Removal Act of 1830'.

A man called Davy Crockett, spoke against such an act. Davy Crockett was already known as an American folk hero, frontiersman, soldier, and politician. He was referred to as *"King of the Wild Frontier".* He represented Tennessee in the US House of Representatives and lost his life in the Texas Revolution at the Battle of the Alamo.

Public Domain Image

During the 'Trail of Tears' an estimated 60,000 Native Americans, African slaves, and white spouses making up to approximately 21,000 Muscogee (Creek), 16,000 Cherokee, 12,500 Choctaw, 6,000 Chickasaw and 4,200 Seminole were forced to use the Trail of Tears.

The various tribes were literally forced, at gun point, from their well-established homes and farms where they had assimilated into the white man's ways and lived as the white man did. But this made no difference as their success led to the need for this fertile land by the white man.

Farms and homes were destroyed to ensure that there was nothing for them to remain for and the Trail of Tears started.

And the various tribes travelled different routes but it all led to the same destination. The Indian Territory in Oklahoma or for many it had meant, death from starvation, mistreatment, or the extreme elements they faced with the weather they had to travel through, without sufficient clothing to protect them and very little food.

The Cherokee have a legend called the *'The Cherokee Rose'*. It's a sad story but it will help you to understand how the Five Civilised Tribes felt when they went through the Trail of Tears and why it was given that name.

The Trail of Tears naturally caused a lot of upset and sadness. Cherokee mothers were helpless to try and help their children survive the harrowing journey, appalling weather conditions and lack of food. And because of this the mothers shed tears.

The elders of the tribe asked for a sign to try and give the mothers the strength they needed to continue, and they got their wish. As the next day dawned, the legend says, a white rose began to grow exactly where the mothers' tears had fallen. The centre of the rose is golden to represent all the gold stolen from the land, and the white petals of the rose itself is said to represent the Cherokee clans.

Public Domain Image

The Cherokee rose still grows along the Trail of Tears route to this day.

By 1837, the Indian Removal Act was almost completed and the bulk of the Five Civilised Tribes were now how housed on the Indian Territory. This then opened up around 25 million acres of more land for white settlers.

anonymous (https://commons.wikimedia.org/wiki/File:Okterritory.png) Okterritory, https://creativecommons.org/licenses/by-sa/3.0/legalcode

THE ALAMO

In the year of 1836, there was a monumental event in the Texas Revolution. The Battle of the Alamo (23rd February – 6th March 1836).

Ch1902
https://commons.wikimedia.org/wiki/File:Wpdms_republic_of_texas.svg
Wpdms republic of texas
https://creativecommons.org/licenses/by-sa/3.0/legalcode

The battle brought together some of the most well-known names of men in history, James Bowie, William B. Travis and Davy Crockett.

The Alamo was originally a home for Spanish missionaries and it was called the Mission San Antonio de Valero. Time changed things as usual and it became a fort for Spanish soldiers who called it the 'Alamo'.

'It consisted of about 3 acres of land surrounded with a 12 foot adobe wall (a wall made from 'sods' of very thick prairie grass). Inside the walls there was a chapel, a barracks for soldiers, a hospital room, a large courtyard, and a horse corral. Along the walls, cannons were placed appropriately for defence.' Wikipedia

American settlers soon started to arrive in San Antonio around the 1820s and by 1821 Mexico had won its independence from Spain. But Texas was part of Mexico and had a government similar to the US Government.

This brought more American settlers into the area wanting to become Mexican citizens.

Public Domain Image

Public Domain Image

James Bowie

Public Domain Image

William B. Travis

Public Domain Image

Davy Crockett

'The Texas Revolution (2ⁿᵈ October, 1835 – 21ˢᵗ April,1836) was a rebellion of colonists from the United States and Tejanos (Hispanic Texans) in putting up armed resistance to the centralist government of Mexico.' Wikipedia

The Texans rebelled against the government changes which were called the *"Siete Leyes"* or *'Seven Laws'* which were a series of constitutional changes that fundamentally altered the organizational structure of Mexico. These changes gave the Mexican National Government and President General Antonio Lopez de Santa Anna almost total power.

Public Domain Image

President General Antonio Lopez de Santa Anna

Months previously in October 1835 Texans had driven all Mexican troops out of Mexican Texas and formed a garrison at the Alamo. This was called The Texas Revolution and started at the Battle of Gonzales. But the garrison was still just a small mission near San Antonio de Bexar.

The Mexican Government believed that the US Government had instigated the Texas insurrection with a goal of seizing the territory. Mexican Congress then passed the *'Tornel Decree'* which meant that anyone fighting against Mexican troops would be *"deemed pirates and dealt with as such, being citizens of no nation presently at war with the Republic and fighting under no recognized flag."*

James Bowie, had originally been sent to destroy the mission so that there was nothing for Santa Anna to find, but instead as one of the commanders there along with Colonel James C. Neill, said in a letter to Governor Henry Smith*, "the salvation of Texas depends in great measure on keeping Bexar out of the hands of the enemy. It serves as the frontier picquet guard, and if it were in the possession of Santa Anna, there is no stronghold from which to repel him in his march to Sabine."* A picquet guard is a soldier, or small unit of soldiers, placed on a defensive line forward of a friendly position to provide timely warning and screening against an enemy advance.

He finished his letter by saying, *"Colonel Neill and myself have come to the solemn resolution that we will rather die in these ditches than give it up to the enemy."*

On 3rd February, William B. Travis arrived with about 30 men. Later Davy Crockett and a group of his volunteers arrived.

In the meantime General Santa Anna had been recruiting for help too, and his army was in the region of just under 7,000.

On 23rd February, 1836 about 1,500 Mexican arrived and occupied San Antonio de Bexar, near the Alamo Mission, with the intention of reclaiming Texas, and they raised the blood-red flag meaning 'no quarter'. No explanation needed. And the battle for possession of the Alamo started.

The two armies fought doggedly and casualties happened but were minimal at that time. Travis knew that the garrison was unprepared for such a continued onslaught from General Santa Anna, and desperately tried to increase the numbers of Texans by writing letters to gain more men and much needed supplies from Texas and the US. He succeeded in gaining a few extra men but the US Government was unwilling to go against the treaty they had with Mexico. By supplying men to fight and supplies to sustain them would have appeared as an act of war. Sam Houston was approached for help but Houston could not spare the men or supplies. They were on their own.

The Texans rebelled against his control and declared their independence on 2nd of March, 1836.

During the start of 6th March, 1836, the Mexican army advanced on the Alamo. The Texans were able to fight successfully against two attacks but the third attack was too much for such a small force of extremely brave and fearless men.

The Mexican army scaled the walls and the Texans continued fighting as they moved inside the walls themselves. Many were killed by the Mexican cavalry as they tried to escape. Some may have tried to surrender, but General Santa Anna's instructions were clear to his men. Take no prisoners.

The last Texan group to remain outside belonged to Davy Crockett, defending a low wall in front of the church. Not able to reload, they used their rifles as clubs and fought with knives too. Valiantly.

Public Domain Image

James Bowie, in hospital at the time, is said to have fought from his bed and probably died there too, killed with a Mexican bayonet. Despite the fact that all the Texans were now dead, the Mexican soldiers continued to either shoot or bayonet dead bodies. Mexican soldiers' bodies were buried in the local cemetery in Campo Santa while the Texan bodies were stacked and burned and the ashes were left to land where they fell.

A simple coffin was filled with the ashes from the funeral pyre and inscribed with the names of Bowie, Crockett and Travis. No one knows exactly where although a coffin was apparently found in 1936, but historians say that it is unlikely to have been their remains.

Public Domain Image

There was one survivor, Susanna Dickinson, who was sent out of the Alamo by the Mexicans to tell everyone of their victory.

The defeat at the Alamo had been very bad for the Texans, but on 21st April, 1836, Houston's army won a battle against the Mexican forces at the Battle of San Jacinto and gained independence for Texas. General Santa Anna was captured the next day and the Mexican army retreated ending the Texas Revolution. During this battle the Texans were inspired to fight on with the now famous cry of *'REMEMBER THE ALAMO'*.

Texas was now an independent colony and later joined the United States. The bill was signed by President Polk on 29th December, 1845, and Texas became the 28th state of the Union formally accepted on 19th February, 1846.

In 1960, John Wayne produced, directed and starred in the film *'The Alamo'* and he said this in an interview in the extras of the film*, "The men who fought here. How can you measure a man? You measure courage and human dignity and a desire for freedom. Well how close we came to those men you will have to decide when you see the version of the story Americans have been telling for six generations. Telling forever."*

gillfoto
https://commons.wikimedia.org/wiki/File:Alamo_Memorial_16L.jpg
https://creativecommons.org/licenses/by-sa/4.0/legalcode

THE GOLD RUSH

Public Domain Image

THE GOLD RUSH

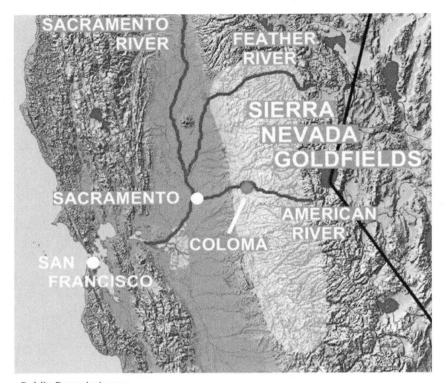

Public Domain Image

Suddenly 1848 saw a huge influx of people arriving in California. Why was this? It was GOLD.

A man, named James W. Marshall, found gold on the 24th January, 1848, at Sutter's Mill in Coloma, California, and the gold rush began. James was building a saw-mill for John Sutter when he found shiny flakes of gold in the river. He told John Sutter about the discovery and they tried to keep it secret. That didn't work and the secret was out and printed in a newspaper, The New York Herald, on 19th August, 1848. And the news spread like wild fire.

Gold seekers homed into the area bringing in about 300,000 people to California from the rest of the United States and abroad. All hoping to make their fortune. And why not?

Blank_US_Map.svg: User:Theshibboleth derivative work: Mangoman88 (talk)
https://commons.wikimedia.org/wiki/File:Emigrant_trails_-_Various_emigrant_trails_showing_California_gold_fields.svg
Emigrant trails - Various emigrant trails showing California gold fields
https://creativecommons.org/licenses/by-sa/3.0/legalcode

Sections of what became the route of the California Trail (an off shoot of the Oregon Trail), discovered and developed by American fur traders including Kit Carson, Joseph R. Walker, and Jedediah Smith, became the route to the gold. Many travellers would utilise the various trails to get where they wanted to go. In the early part of 1848 the numbers of people living there was around 800. This increased dramatically later that year to 20,000 then a huge jump in population by the end of 1848 with a total of about 100,000. Everyone seemed to want to be in California. Travelling by sea or by land just to get near the area.

Many men already living in San Francisco abandoned the area to also seek their fortune leaving the city almost free of males. But the mining towns that developed around California because of the gold rush, still had San Francisco at their heart for supplies and gold exchange.

Through 1849 thousands of people arrived to hunt for gold and they were given the nickname of the 'Forty Niners'. They arrived after horrendous journeys to get there with some having to leave their families behind, probably in debt due to the need for gold seeking equipment. They were looking for their dream of wealth and many left their wives and children to fend for themselves.

And they came from all over the world, China, Mexico, Europe and even Australia.

Public Domain Image

Gold had been fairly easy to find as it was surface gold. The gold miners could 'pan' for the gold. But by 1850 this had really started to disappear. But they still kept coming. The gold rush helped in the making of California into the 31st state in September 1850. This brought more people into the area.

Finding gold was not an easy job to start with and if you struck it rich then you were just in the right place at the right time. There was no real skill involved. But you had to put the work in first.

As gold became harder and harder to find, mining became an industry instead and technology took over. Hydraulic mining had taken over. This is a form of mining that uses high-pressure jets of water to dislodge rock material or move sediment. The course of rivers had been forced to alter, as water dams were needed for the hydraulic mine sites themselves and this took the water away from nearby farmlands.

By 1853 mining had found gold again but it had also destroyed the landscape. The source of gold started to decline and by 1855 it had almost gone. But the miners stayed and the area became hugely populated. They tried many ways to extract gold from the ground and the success and determination to find gold continued.

The gold rush officially ended in 1855.

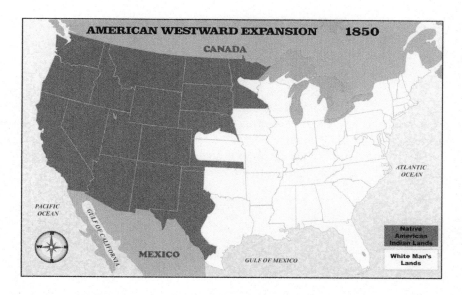

PIKES PEAK GOLD RUSH

Just a few years later, Pikes Peak Gold Rush in 1858 – 1861 (also known as the Colorado Gold Rush) brought about 100,000 prospectors into the Kansas/Nebraska territory all looking to become rich. These prospectors were to become known as 'fifty-niners' after 1859 and the gold rush even had its own motto of *'Pikes Peak or Bust'!*

Pikes Peak Gold Rush quickly followed the California Gold Rush and became one of the greatest gold rushes there was of the time. As with other gold mining towns, Pikes Peak generated the start of two large camps that were to become Denver City and Boulder City. Smaller ones disappeared as the prospectors moved on.

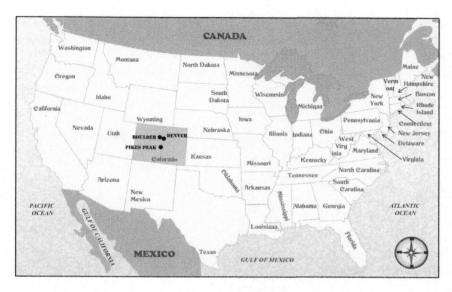

It was thought that there was an abundance of gold in and around Colorado but nothing substantial had been found although trappers and gold seeking parties panned for gold as they travelled. One trapper is said to have found the ultimate fortune in gold specimens when he took what he had found into New Mexico. He could have been a very rich man, if he could have remembered where he had found the gold specimens in the first place that is. Poor soul.

Public Domain Image

But the quest for gold continued, even after California Gold Rush had ended and many had returned home disheartened. It wasn't long before a party of prospectors working the Southern Platte River near Cherry Creek near what is now known as Denver, found gold and started the gold rush again. Prospectors faced all kinds of weather to get there before everyone else.

Shannon1
https://commons.wikimedia.org/wiki/File:South_Platte_basin_map.png
https://creativecommons.org/licenses/by-sa/4.0/legalcode

The rush was over by 1861 but quite a few prospectors had become rich.

THE GROWTH OF BOOMTOWNS

Boomtowns suddenly appeared to cater for the miners, (and buffalo hunters), every possible need and gave them the opportunity to spend their gold and cash on items at very high prices.

Boomtowns would usually start out as just a few tents, growing very quickly as word got out about gold and many prospectors would arrive to seek their fortune and swell the numbers. Sometimes the boomtowns literally grew overnight.

Usually a general store would appear plus other shops where you could buy almost anything you might needed at exorbitant prices. Selling tools to the miners and new prospectors gave the store owners huge profits. If you needed the equipment then you paid the prices. The store owners became very rich men very quickly.

Buildings were erected very quickly and not usually of very good quality. Just sufficient to get a kind of roof over your head while you were there. There was no law and order. Just the order of the gun. If you had one, use it. If you didn't you were dead and someone could take your claim.

Public Domain Image
Deadwood

Public Domain Image
Deadwood

Restaurants, hotels, saloons and gambling gave the miners, buffalo hunters, cardsharps and prospectors another way to spend their money.

Some spending or losing it all and having to go back out there to find more gold if at all possible.

Hotels were a rare luxury, particularly if your bed had been under the stars and open to the elements for some considerable time. Even if it meant you had to share with a stranger. It was still a bed and indoors!

With any new settlement or boomtown one of the first premises built, probably a large tent, would be a gambling hall. As the population grew, the gambling halls became the largest and most decorative buildings there with the most necessary bar, a stage for the dancing girls, and hotel rooms for guests.

If you had more than one gambling hall and professional gamblers, then the boomtown was a success. It meant money and lots of it for the owners. It had a nickname too. If a boomtown allowed gambling then it would be called 'wide awake' or 'wide open'. Professional gamblers rented their own tables in a gambling hall and they had to have a reputation for fair play, and having a straight game. They were called 'sports' and they didn't drink, cheat or swear.

Cattle towns in Texas, Oklahoma, Kansas, and Nebraska became famous centres for gambling. Cowhands with money to burn after a long and arduous drive had money to gamble with.

Abilene, Dodge City, Wichita, Omaha and Kansas City all approved and encouraged gambling. But this could also lead to trouble. Law enforcement tended to be more stringent in towns than in rural areas. Law enforcement was there to maintain peace rather than engaging in face to face shoot-outs. Drunkenness, disarming rowdy cowhands who disregarded the gun laws of the town and any problems that might occur during gambling or prostitution disputes were the usual kinds of trouble.

But whenever gold was discovered in a new place, the miners would move on quickly abandoning the boomtown and establishing another somewhere else. A lot of boomtowns soon became 'ghost towns'.

The cities of San Francisco and Columbia are two examples of boomtowns during the California Gold Rush. Columbia was founded as a boomtown in 1850 when gold was found nearby and was known as the "Gem of the Southern Mines."

Fortune seekers arrived in wagons, clipper ships and even on horseback staking claims on land around the river 'panning' for gold in the silt from the river itself. Even some of the crews on-board ships arriving in San Francisco abandoned their jobs to join the gold rush leaving boats to rot over time, or to be used as accommodation for those seeking the gold, as they were converted into temporary accommodation.

Public Domain Image

Public Domain Image

Shrewd business men decided that they needed to make the most out of the wealth generated by the gold rush. The banking industry, even then, was on a winning streak. The founding of Wells Fargo in 1852 brought two men together. Henry Wells and William G. Fargo, who had already started express companies in their own names. Wells founded Wells and Company, while Fargo was a partner in the Livingston, Fargo and Company.

In 1849 another business had the same idea of express delivery. John Warren Butterfield founded Butterfield, Wasson & Company. But it seemed like they were wasting time competing against each other for the same financial rewards, and decided on a more positive approach and in 1850 they formed the American Express Company, now more popularly known by many, as the credit card company American Express.

But the gold rush in California seemed to be the best place to be for business profits. A firm called Adams and Company had already begun to establish themselves in the gold rush area and with opposition from the directors of the American Express Company, Wells and Fargo decided to strike out in another business in 1852. Wells Fargo.

WELLS FARGO

Wells Fargo had originally acted as an express service to ship the gold from San Francisco to New York City. Stagecoaches were used taking the gold straight to steamships for transportation.

Wells Fargo was also an American banking company based in San Francisco, California. Gold miners were some of the first customers to use the bank during the gold rush. But in the Panic of 1855, Wells Fargo had to face its first financial crisis when the Californian banking system collapsed due to some financial speculation that was unsuccessful. Wells Fargo, after a run on the bank of Page, Bacon & Company, had to close its doors too.

But not for long as they had forward planned, and were able to survive the Panic of 1855, as they had sufficient assets there to meet their customers' demands. This stood them in good stead after the Panic as the over 200 businesses had folded giving Wells Fargo the opportunity to gain importance within San Francisco. But more importantly, Wells Fargo had gained a good reputation of being dependable.

Marine 69-71
https://commons.wikimedia.org/wiki/File:Apache_Junction-Superstition_Mountain_Museum-Wells_Fargo_Bank.JPG
https://creativecommons.org/licenses/by-sa/4.0/legalcode

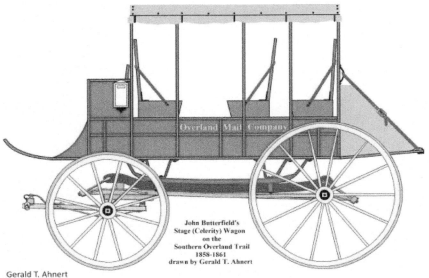

John Butterfield's
Stage (Celerity) Wagon
on the
Southern Overland Trail
1858-1861
drawn by Gerald T. Ahnert

Gerald T. Ahnert
https://commons.wikimedia.org/wiki/File:Butterfield's_Stage_(Celerity)_Wagon.jpg)
https://creativecommons.org/licenses/by-sa/4.0/legalcode

Their success continued and they were able to develop their stage coach business, taking over the Butterfield Overland Mail service and were part of the Pony Express during its last six months of operation.

PONY EXPRESS

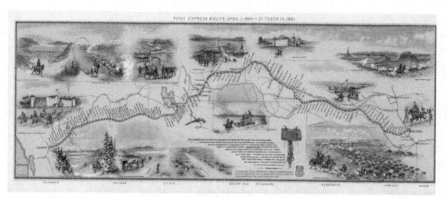

Public Domain Image

The Pony Express was a mail service delivering messages, newspapers, and mail using a variety of horse riders covering between Missouri and California. It was only in operation for 18 months but its success was the speed in which messages were delivered, and became the most direct way to communicate.

The route used was a hard one and over the route itself there were approximately 190 stations. These stations were essential and the station keepers ensured that the whole operation ran smoothly by ensuring that fresh horses/riders were there to carry on the task quickly and efficiently.

The Pony Express employed about 80 riders with 400 other staff spread out over the various stations tending stock or supervising routes. The riders had to be skilled riders and movies and books have epitomised them as American heroes. And why not as it was a pretty dangerous job riding through the territory in those days.

Public Domain Image

**Pony Express Riders
'Billy' Richardson, Johnny Fry,
Charles Cliff and Gus Cliff**

Sadly the Pony Express was not a success financially and they went bankrupt after about 18 months.

Until the telegraph and the railroads arrived about in 1861 and everything changed.

Public Domain Image

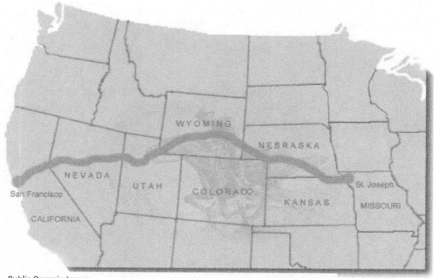

Public Domain Image

Pony Express Route

RAILROADS – BUFFALO HUNTING

In the 1860s the railways started to become prominent and by 1869 the Transcontinental Railroad linked East with West, and helped settlers 'fill in the blanks' in the wide open territory that was now available.

Public Domain Image

The railways were given millions of acres of 'free land', 175 million acres to be precise, to encourage not only the railways to build their lines, but also to enabled them to make a huge profit selling this land onto the settlers.

The land they were promoting in the West was called an 'uninhabited paradise' and it was up for grabs. Each parcel of land sold, even as small as about 50 acres, gave each new potential settler a fantastic opportunity to start a new life. The land was so very cheap it must have felt like it was too good to be true. But even that thought didn't put them off. Life was going to be good for the settlers from now on.

All along the route of the rail lines, boomtowns sprung up and stayed for as long as the railway was there. It was somewhere for the rail-workers to live, to spend their hard earned cash and gain a bit of R & R too.

But they needed feeding. And what does every hard working railway man need to keep him going? Well buffalo meat was the ideal food.

And it became a railway practise to hire experienced (or inexperienced) buffalo hunters to use their skills with the rifle to help fill this need for buffalo meat.

And they too came in droves, as there was a lot of money to be made from buffalo hunting. The demand for buffalo meat continued from the railway workers as the railroad continued its expansion. Because of this demand the slaughter continued adding to the fame and legend of hunters like Buffalo Bill Cody who was hired by the railroad for this purpose. Buffalo Bill earned about $500 a month (about $11,624 today).

Public Domain Image

Public Domain Image

The railroads also came up with a brilliant idea for more profit for themselves, and that was to sell sporting trips. Trips where, from the safety of your cabin, nobility from England or wherever could shoot buffalo.

This proved to be a very popular sport, and the participants were allowed to bring their trophies back with them, a tongue, a buffalo head, a hide to hang on their wall at home, while the rest of the dead animal was just left to rot and the Native America to starve.

Meat sales started to decline once the railway was completed, but the hides became a resource instead. In 1870 someone came up with a new tanning idea which meant there was more money to be made by turning the hides into good quality leather. The race was on again to make big bucks.

Restaurants had also found a new popular delicacy in the shape of buffalo tongues. This meant that the buffalo hunters were again able to make very easy money gaining 50 cents per tongue.

The tongues were smoked and salted then shipped back in barrels to the various restaurants to sell to their diners for an exorbitant fee. The hunters and the restaurant owners were rolling in it.

Public Domain Image

A new rail head in Kansas in a place called Dodge City was the ideal place for the hides and tongues to be sent to and shipped out. While the rest of the slaughtered carcass was left where it fell just to rot.

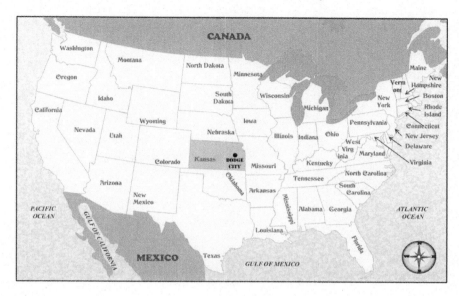

Dodge City started like many other boomtowns, as an outpost called Fort Dodge on the Santa Fe Trail in 1865. It was somewhere for the wagon trains and the post riders to find shelter and protection from 'Indian' attacks.

It developed very simply from a three bedroomed 'sod house' built by a settler called Henry L. Stiller on his cattle ranch near to the fort. It wasn't long before buffalo hunters and traders stayed there which encouraged Stiller to open a whiskey bar, then to open a store, a dance hall, a restaurant, a barber shop and a smithy. And Dodge City was born.

Buffalo hunters and quite a few cattle rustlers had money to spend but they brought along their own kind of rough and ready behaviour and somewhat offensive 'out of doors' aromas that were attached to the various roles they had.

But rumour has it that if you got too rowdy and couldn't hold your drink, then Dodge City had the perfect solution to cover this. It was a 15 foot well, and that's where you were placed, unceremoniously, and left there until you sobered up.

During my research I found what is described as a 'fun fact' and I suppose it depends on your point of view, but here goes. When the employees from the railway arrived in Dodge City, they were in need of some female company. A place called 'China Doll' was a favourite place to visit and the men would carry red caboose (railcar) lanterns to see their way there in the unlit streets of Dodge City lighting their way with a red glow. This is apparently where the term 'red light district' came from. Now you know.

Anonymous
https://commons.wikimedia.org/wiki/File:CNW_brakeman's_kerosene_lantern.JPG
CNW brakeman's kerosene lantern
https://creativecommons.org/licenses/by-sa/2.0/legalcode

But Dodge City proved to be a 'dream come true' for the buffalo hunters too. There was easy money to make and the demand was high. And as the buffalo themselves, seemed to be such stupid animals, easy to kill, then it was very easy money. Buffalo have very poor vision and if they saw an animal killed next to them, they didn't run away in panic, they just stood there and had a good look before moving on.

Therefore one shooter with a long-range rifle could drop 50-100 head of buffalo without much effort or panic within the herd.

A renowned hunter called Tom Nixon is reported to have shot 120 animals in 40 minutes. He continued his 'record' in 1873 when he slaughtered 3,200 in 35 days, which beat Buffalo Bill Cody's record of killing 4,280 in 18 months making Cody's record pale in comparison. *"Kill every buffalo you can! Every buffalo dead is an Indian gone."* This was the simple rule the hunters were given by a Colonel (unknown) and they followed this rule happily. If there were no buffalo then the Indians would have to move away. Simple logic from the white man.

During the winter of 1871–72 a single buffalo hide was worth $3.50. The equivalent of about $95 in this day and age. A fortune for those hunting. Within two years the hunters, working mainly the Kansas plains, were rich men. But by the spring of 1874 buffalo herds had all but disappeared. The buffalo hunters easy money became a lot less easy to make and the competition was great.

Public Domain Image

One scout travelling from Dodge City to the Indian Territory said, *'In 1872 we were never out of sight of the buffalo. In the following autumn, while travelling over the same district, the whole country was whitened with bleached and bleaching bones.'*

Public Domain Image

This forced the buffalo hunters to move further afield to hunt the buffalo to meet demands and to make more money. So they headed south to the Texas plains, where there were huge herds, and the money started to land back into the hands of the buffalo hunters again. Everything that they had hoped for. And the slaughter continued.

No one seemed too worried about the consequences of all the buffalo hunting and the depletion of the buffalo itself. They were following the instructions sent out of 'kill every buffalo you can' and they were making a pretty penny too. What was there to worry about? This too was part of the 'Manifest Destiny' to deprive the Native Americans of their principal food supply.

Public Domain Image

General Phil Sheridan came up with a much better explanation by saying, *'These men [hunters] have done in the last two years . . . more to settle the vexed Indian question than the entire regular army has done in the last thirty years,'* he said, *'They are destroying the Indians' commissary . . . For the sake of a lasting peace, let them kill, skin and sell until the buffaloes are exterminated. Then your prairies can be covered with speckled cattle and the festive cowboy.'*

Today, some 20,000-25,000 buffalo remain in public herds. And soon the prairies did become *'covered with speckled cattle and the festive cowboy'*.

COWBOYS AND CATTLE DRIVES

Public Domain Image

COWBOYS AND CATTLE DRIVES

Cowboys have, and always will be, immortalised in books and movies as American heroes. Movies are still being made on this theme and John Wayne, and actors like him, have paved the way for this fascinating topic to be explored.

A cowboy, or cowhand, of the Old West always rode 'tall in his saddle' on his trusty horse. And he would have to be a good rider too. He would also probably be aged between 16-30 years old and make about $1 per day with possibly a long wait until the end of the cattle drive to gain his pay.

But he would be working in brutal weather and long, long hours of very hard work. Ever wary of the dangers that the land they travelled on could bring, including snakes, scorpions, lack of water, lack of shelter, not to forget the bedbugs and the lice.

But the name itself is a bit of an insult really. Yes they were boys that tended cows, but in some circles it's said that calling him a 'cowboy' meant that he was the worst kind of outlaw or desperado. What they really should be called is cattle men, cow pokes, cowhands, drovers and it was when dime novels were written about them that the name changed to cowboy.

But it wasn't all cattle drives. Before a drive, one of the cowhand's jobs was to ride out onto the range and gather the scattered cattle back to the ranch. The best cattle would be selected, roped, and branded, and most male cattle were castrated. They were called steers now.

They did have other duties before this on the ranch such as fixing fences and add this to the long boring times of nothingness until the cattle were ready for the drives, and it doesn't sound all that much fun for not a lot of cash either.

But the drives themselves took months to do covering hundreds of miles, in searing heat and riding about 14 hours each day.

Cattle drives that included using the *Shawnee Trail (San Antonio – Missouri 1840s – 1867)*, the *Chisholm Trail (Texas –Kansas railheads 1867-1884)*, the *Great Western Cattle Trail* (also known as *Fort Griffin Trail, Dodge City Trail* or *Texas Trail, 1874-1885)* and the *Goodnight-Loving Trail (Fort Belknap, Texas – Denver-Wyoming, 1866-1867)*. Hundreds of thousands of longhorn cattle were driven on these trails to be shipped to markets across the United States.

But the cattle drive itself was not a straight forward operation. There was a huge demand for the cattle and obviously the owner wanted them at their destination as quickly as possible to gain his payment per head. But there was also a need to keep the cattle at a good marketable weight. Run them too hard and too quickly and they would lose their weight and would be difficult to sell at the end of the trail itself. A day in the life of the long horn could be as much as 25 miles. This could cause weight loss problems if continued.

So some cattle drives travelled shorter distances each day, about 15 miles, and also allowed a bit of R & R for the cattle a couple of times during the day to rest and eat. This helped the cattle to maintain their start weight. More profit at the end of the trail.

But it also meant it was a slower journey as the trails could take months to complete. The Chisholm Trail from the ranch to the railhead was one of the most important trails. It led from near Fort Worth, Texas, through Indian Territory (Oklahoma) to the railhead in Abilene.

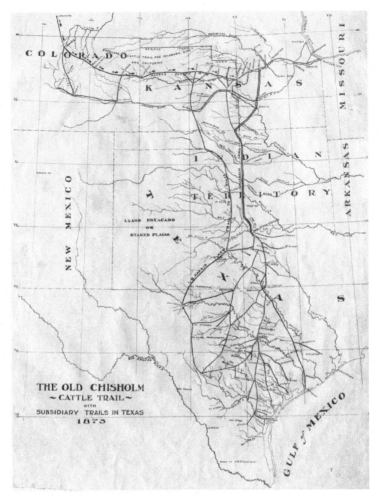

Public Domain Image

But a need arose to try to avoid farm settlements on the trail as a disease in the long horn cattle called 'tick fever' started to cause trouble. Farmers did not want to see cattle drives crossing their lands in-case the disease was carried by the long horn cattle and passed onto their stock as they grazed.

The California Gold Rush in the 1850s created a huge demand for beef. If you had the gold to pay for it that is! This created long cattle drives from Mexico sending shipments of beef to San Francisco using the new freezing methods even sending beef over to Britain too. It was imperative that the cattle drives continued.

By 1853 farmers started to block cattle drives of long horns going through their land to try and stop the spread of 'Texas Fever'. Longhorns were immune but not so the stock on the farm. By 1855 farmers in Missouri had formed vigilante groups to stop the herds and kill the cattle that came near. A law came into effect to protect the farmers and banning the herds travelling through the area, so the drovers moved over to Kansas, but met the same resistance there too.

'In 1867 a young Illinois livestock dealer, Joseph G. McCoy, built market facilities at Abilene, Kansas, at the end of the Chisholm Trail. The new route to the west of the Shawnee soon began carrying the bulk of the Texas herds, leaving the earlier trail to dwindle for a few years and expire.' Wikipedia

Cowhands worked in shifts on a cattle drive, to watch the cattle 24 hours a day, herding them in the proper direction in the daytime and watching them at night to prevent stampedes and deter theft. During a cattle drive there would be about 1,500–2,500 head of cattle. Those involved in the drive would probably have been the owner in charge, from ten – fifteen 'hands' each of them with five – ten horses, and a 'horse wrangler' who tended all the horses. He was usually a very young boy. Most necessary was a cook who would be a very well respected member of the team with lots of experience on a cattle drive. He not only made sure that they were all fed but he also knew a bit about how to fix you if you got hurt and would carry some form of medical supplies just in-case. He also drove the chuck wagon.

The chuck wagon held, not only the meat, beans, bacon and coffee and all the necessary supplies for the journey, but also the bed rolls for the cowhands. The cook would probably bake bread, if he had the necessary to do this, and the cattle ate on the hoof as they had to be kept in tip top condition for the sale.

Cowhands were paid about $1 per day but not until the cattle were sold at the end of the drive. So it was their responsibility to get them there on time and in a good saleable weight for the best profits.

Abilene had been the place to head for until it lost its status as a shipping point for cattle, making the Chisholm Trail not so important anymore either in 1871. Dodge City became the place to head for. That is until the Atchison, Topeka and Santa Fe Railway arrived making the Chisholm Trail important again for driving Texas cattle north to market.

Public Domain Image

Cowhands didn't really want adventure on the trail though as this meant that it came in the form of Native Americans attacking or cattle rustlers, and the ever changing weather including freak thunder storms that would spook the cattle into a stampede. Which meant then you had to go and find them again after the storm and herd them up again. Wherever they were.

A cowhand had to have a good relationship with his horse and also be a good horseman. Roping a steer (castrated cattle) was a skill too, as it didn't take much to lose a finger if you roped a steer wrongly and it kept on running with you still attached.

And you had to be able to sing. Something soft though just to settle the cattle and not spook them into a panic. No 'yippy ki yay' tunes or you could lose the herd very quickly as they ran from the noise.

68

Public Domain Image

Cowhands were cowhands for years, sometimes never seeing a razor touch their faces nor dressing up in a nice shirt and necktie. By the time they reached their destination at the railhead, after months of boring repetitive work, awful repetitive food (beans, beans and more beans) your pay in your hand at the end of the drive, cowhands were more than ready for a bath, a shave and a haircut, new clothes, a bit of nocturnal adventure if you get my drift, sipping whisky or a fair few beers and perhaps even a good night's sleep. It was a 'rip roaring' time they had in the local cattle town and sometimes it could turn a bit violent.

And this saw the introduction of the 'peace officer' who came in the shape of a few famous names such as James Butler Hickok, Wyatt Earp and Bat Masterson. These three were the best known cattle town marshals.

Theodore Roosevelt said of the cowhand, *"He lives in the lonely lands where mighty rivers in long reaches between the barren bluffs where the prairies stretch out on billowy plains of lush grass. Only the blue horizon on the plains across whose endless breath he can steer his course for days or weeks, and see neither man to speak to nor hill to break the view.*

Where the glory of the burning splendour of the sunset kindle the blue vaults of heaven and the level brown earth till they merge together in an ocean of flaming fire."

In the 1880s the cattle boom was over. Many of the herds were decimated during the 1886-1887 winters with temperatures of minus 46. One storm lasted for 10 days. Some 66% of cattle were lost as the animals could not find a way around the barbed wire fences. Cowhands and settlers alike died of exposure during this time.

The cattle drives had run their course and after a successful couple of decades disappeared as the railroads and refrigeration took over.

Sheep grazing was tried too when the cattle ranching came to an end. But Americans were not really mutton eaters. Although popular in 1867, it appears to have declined. Many disapproved of sheep farming and this led to many a sheep farmer being injured or killed if he continued to let his sheep graze on the lush land.

Ranches became areas covered with barbed wire, invented by Joseph Glidden in 1867, to stop cattle from roaming freely keeping the stock together. This sounds like a good idea but it just brought conflict as water rights started disputes creating fence cutting wars as homesteaders wanted their cattle to roam free and have use of the water and the land. As scholar Susanne Bentley puts it, barbed wire *"closed off land, closed people in, and enabled some people to acquire land illegally."*

Smaller holdings of cattlemen, opposed the closing of the open range, and began cutting barbed wire fences to allow cattle to pass through to find grazing land. This led to conflict with many vigilantes joining which caused chaos and even death.

'The Fence Cutting Wars ended in 1884 making fence cutting a felony. An 1885 a federal law was passed banning such fences across the public domain.' Wikipedia

Barbed wire is said by historians as the 'invention that tamed the West. Controlling cattle on the open range required a lot of manpower, particularly catching strays and bringing them back to the herd. Barbed wire solved this as it was cheap and easy to erect making it the ideal way to control the movement of cattle by fencing them in. But it did lead to the end of cowhands being needed and by the start of the 20th Century they were not required. Thankfully they will always be a part of American history and a part of the Old West that is now immortalised in movies.

PROGRESS

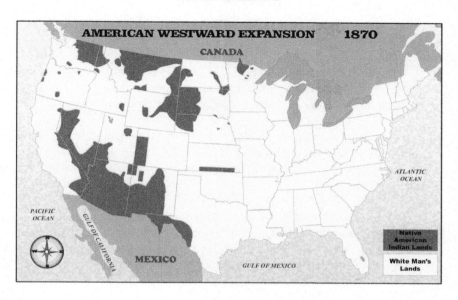

PROGRESS

All this was happening and the American Nation was booming. There were huge technological changes and with the coming of the railroad this virtually ended the Santa Fe and Oregon Trails.

With the growing number of immigrants arriving into America all seeking their fortunes in this wondrous land, it had meant a huge number of extra mouths needed feeding. And it helped develop and increase the new industry. Cattle.

Railroads meant cattle. Cattle was big business. Millions of acres of land, Native American land, were used by cattle barons with ranches all over the area and with ever expanding herds of cattle. Thousands upon thousands of them, all helping to fuel the growth of America.

Texans made fortunes with their epic cattle drives to railheads to sell their cattle quicker into Chicago markets via the trains. Life was good for the white man. Things were really looking up.

Buffalo hunters now had a much quicker way of getting their 'booty' to market and make their money quicker too.

The coming of the railroad had literally brought everything together and everyone in some way or another felt the impact of this huge technological change. And I do mean everybody.

But there was still one hurdle left to overcome. The Great Plains Indian tribes had to be dealt with. They were holding up this important progress.

ESTABLISHMENT OF FORTS

As the settlers moved constantly westward, established US Military forts moved with them. They were there to maintain order over the new territories. They served their purpose as bases for any military action needed against the Native American, or for nearby assistance if needed by settlers or troops.

Fort Bowie was there to protect Apache Pass in Arizona as this was the mail route between Tucson and El Paso. This meant that the soldiers there would encounter such Apache warriors as Cochise and Geronimo.

Fort Laramie and Fort Kearny ultimately protected any of the settlers' wagon trains passing through the Great Plains with other outposts in California set up to protect the miners.

Protecting the miners was essential on the Sioux lands as they, naturally, objected to the miners digging up the gold in their sacred Black Hills. And forts along the railway lines of the Union Pacific helped to try and stave off attacks there too.

'Other important forts were Fort Sill, Oklahoma, Fort Smith, Arkansas, Fort Snelling, Minnesota, Fort Union, New Mexico, Fort Worth, Texas, and Fort Walla Walla in Washington. Fort Omaha, Nebraska. Fort Huachuca in Arizona near to Tombstone, was also originally a frontier post and is still in use by the US Army.' Wikipedia

And many of them encountered, in some way or other, the Native American.

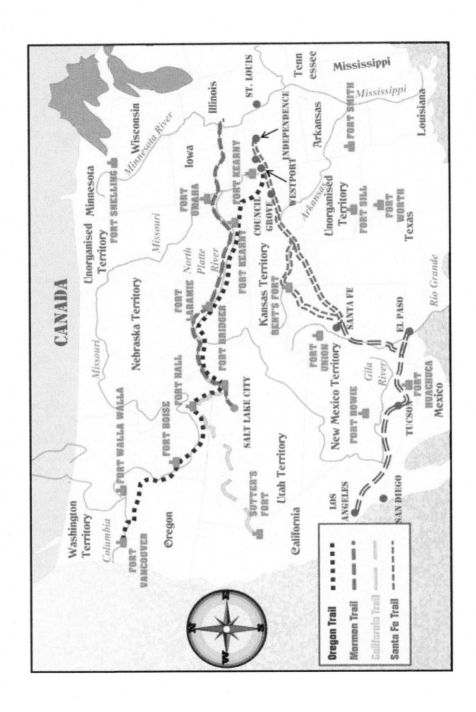

SOME OF THOSE FAMOUS BATTLES

Public Domain Image

FORT LARAMIE

Some of the most famous names in Native American history were still fighting for their lives and traditions during the American expansion.

Skirmishes and battles continued throughout the Native American land and many peace treaties were broken by the US Government and the Native American.

In 1851, in a completely different part of the picture, the US Government was trying to establish peace between themselves and the many tribes within the Wyoming, Dakota, and Montana areas. They established a treaty called the Fort Laramie Treaty of 1851.

But peace with the Native Americans came with a price. The US Government wanted to build roads and forts on the land belonging to the Sioux, with a promise that they would protect the Sioux from the white settlers. They also promised to provide annuities of $50,000 for 50 years. Then they re-thought this and made it 15 years.

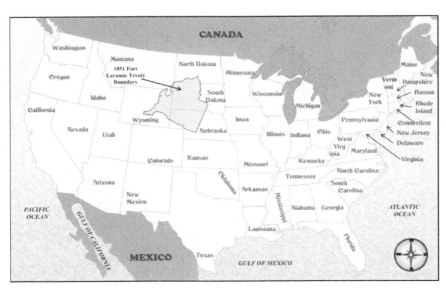

But the treaty caused many a problem for the US Government as the US officials just assumed that the Sioux understood what was going to happen, and as they had 'touched the pen', they therefore must have understood.

Older Sioux leaders did want peace with the white man, but the younger warriors like Sitting Bull, who was twenty two at the time, still wanted the honour of battle, stealing horses from their enemies, the Crow and keeping their land from the white man.

But the treaty was reneged very quickly when gold was found and the settlers and prospectors arrived claiming the land, fencing it off, and killing the buffalo and any other game. Native Americans were starving and many were forced to surrender but many others died fighting back or just trying to stay alive.

GRATTAN MASSACRE

    The constant increase in the white man's numbers and their need for Native American land, led to many a conflict or out and out battle.

The various trails had already been established bringing wagon trains, with settlers, gold miners, basically anyone seeking a new life. And one in particular, the Mormon Trail, brought Mormon settlers down to the Oregon Trail and near to Fort Laramie where a Brulee camp (Sioux) was situated. Their arrival led to what is now known as the Grattan Massacre.

This occurred in 1854 when a very keen young Lieutenant, John L. Grattan, marched his troops into a Brulee village and demanded the surrender of a Miniconjou visitor in Conquering Bear's Sioux camp.

Public Domain Image

The Miniconjou visitor had apparently killed a cow that had strayed from a Mormon wagon train on the Oregon Trail. The Mormons had been passing by Conquering Bear's camp, just outside of Fort Laramie, when the cow had decided to stray. The Mormons had been offered the cow back by Conquering Bear, but not understanding what was being said to them, and the fact that the cow was now in a camp belonging to 'savages', the Mormons left the cow and reported it as stolen to the Fort's commander.

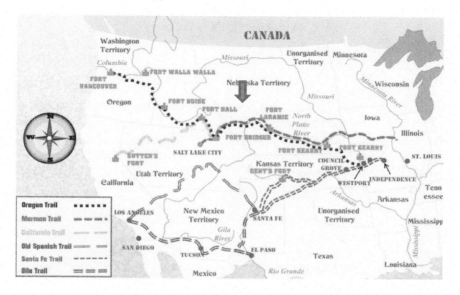

In the meantime the Brulee camp ate well for the first time in ages.

Acting on the Mormons complaint Grattan went to Conquering Bear's camp taking along an interpreter, Lucien Auguste. Auguste was drunk and did nothing other than taunt Conquering Bear and the Sioux instead of translating what was said. This did not help the situation.

Grattan's insistence that the perpetrator be handed over for punishment was never going to happen, as he was a visitor at Conquering Bear's camp. Conquering Bear offered a horse as trade but was refused. Grattan started to leave the camp to give Conquering Bear 'time to change his mind', when a shot rang out and Conquering Bear was dead. Shot whilst walking back to his tipi.

Then Sioux arrows found their targets in retribution and army bullets hit their targets too. Not only was Conquering Bear killed, but all of Grattan's soldiers, Grattan included. It was called the Grattan Massacre and paved the way for many more Sioux battles with the US military and the white man too.

APACHE WARS

The Apache Wars between 1849-1886 involved Mangas Coloradas, Cochise, Geronimo, Victorio and Nana. All highly skilled Apache warriors but against the ever increasing might of the US Army this eventually forced them into surrender as their Apache numbers dwindled with the constant fighting, while the US soldiers numbers just seemed to increase.

Cochise had tried for peace with the white man but the Bascom Affair in 1861 had soured any trust he may have had for them.

Cochise had been blamed for the kidnap of John Ward's 12 year old son. John Ward was a local settler and was adamant that Cochise was behind the kidnap. Although Cochise was not involved at all with this kidnap, Lieutenant George N. Bascom, a man totally inexperienced with any form of dealing with the Native American, was given the task of sorting this out. He failed big style.

Using information he had gathered quickly and incorrectly, and using the fact that Cochise had a good working relationship with the people of the Butterfield Overland Mail Services, he sent out an invite to Cochise for a meeting.

Under the impression that the meeting was a peaceful parley, on 3rd February, 1861, Cochise arrived with some of his family, and was escorted into a tent for refreshments. Then the tent was surrounded by soldiers. Cochise soon realised that the meeting was not the peaceful gesture he thought it would be, particularly as Bascom proceeded to accuse him of the kidnapping and tried to chain him up. It was obvious to Cochise very quickly that he was going to be held as a prisoner.

Cochise was furious and in a struggle managed to cut himself out of the tent and escape. The Apache called this incident *'cut the tent'*. But his family were still being held. Over the course of the next few days, Cochise tried to secure his families release offering to trade the white hostages he had acquired. But Bascom refused. He wanted the boy returned. Cochise took the hostages away.

This attempt at bargaining continued, as did various attacks, but Bascom would not listen to reason, even from his men. They could see no good coming out of this. But Bascom was in charge.

He sent his troops out in search of Cochise and all they found were the dead bodies of the hostages. In retaliation, Bascom hung his hostages, Cochise's brother and his two nephews. Now it was really personal and Cochise needed revenge which he got through many attacks on the soldiers and wagon trains killing anyone that got in the way. The white man had proved that they could not be trusted yet again. And historians say that Bascom's ignorance was to blame for this revenge as he had badly handled the whole Cochise situation. Many people died because of Bascom's actions towards Cochise and if Bascom had handled the situation better they would not have been in that hostage situation and been killed. Whatever view you take, this Bascom Affair triggered more battles.

Just as a point of interest, the alleged kidnapped boy was living happily in an Apache camp as an Apache, nowhere near Cochise and his people. He became an Apache scout when he grew older.

But Cochise soon became very ill and his illness and ultimate death on 8th June, 1874 gave him the only kind of peace that he was likely to get. Geronimo, Victorio and Nana took over the quest to regain their freedom and fought with the US Army and the Mexican Army on many occasions. They were fiercely determined warriors.

Public Domain Image
Mangas Coloradas

Not long after the Bascom Affair in 1863, Mangas Coloradas, an older warrior and mentor to both Cochise and Geronimo, sought peace with the white man. He had led the Apache in many a battle and won. But now it was time to change.

He accepted an invite to parley and the white man's promises sounded good, fair, and acceptable. Mangas agreed to the terms. Cochise and Geronimo refused.

Mangas was so convinced that all would be well that he attended the parley with only a very small number of his tribe. And he was never seen again.

Once he arrived at the parley he was arrested and held under guard 24/7. Brigadier General Joseph R. West wanted him dead. He made that very clear. And during the night he got his wish, as his soldiers adhered to his request by taunting this unarmed, chained man who tried hard to ignore their constant taunts. And while tied up and lying on the ground, Mangas was prodded constantly with red hot bayonets. Mangas tried to sit up to protest and they took this as an attack or an attempt to escape, and shot him in the chest, then in the head saying later that he had become aggressive. To make matters worse they scalped him, cut off his head and boiled it in a pot.

Geronimo and the Apache were incensed by this when they heard of his murder. Cochise and the Chokonen tribe, Geronimo and the Bendonkes warriors from Mangas' tribe joined forces and the battles continued.

Geronimo attempted peace many years later and had many a 'parley' to discuss terms. But the trust was just not there when it came to it. Geronimo felt that the white man would not keep his promises, and the Apache hated liars. Geronimo was not wrong.

Geronimo surrendered and escaped on a quite few occasions until that day on 4th September, 1886 when he finally handed over his rifle to General Nelson A. Miles. He was made a prisoner of war, as was Nana. They and their remaining warriors were imprisoned at Fort Marion until 1894 when they at long last, were reunited with their families and moved to the Kiowa/ Comanche/Apache reservation at Fort Sill along with all the other tribes.

anonymous (https://commons.wikimedia.org/wiki/File:Okterritory.png) Okterritory, https://creativecommons.org/licenses/by-sa/3.0/legalcode

BLACK KETTLE (CHEYENNE)

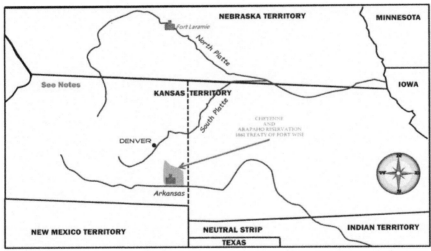

On 29th November, 1864, Black Kettle (Cheyenne) who was a peaceful man, soon realised that he was fighting a losing battle against the military power of the US Army and with the ever increasing encroachment of the white man on their lands, surrendered and accepted the terms of the Treaty of Fort Wise in 1861. Signed sealed and delivered at Fort Lyon.

NEBRASKA TERRITORY

MINNESOTA

Fort Laramie

North Platte

See Notes

IOWA

KANSAS TERRITORY

South Platte

CHEYENNE
AND
ARAPAHO RESERVATION
1861 TREATY OF FORT WISE

DENVER

Arkansas

NEW MEXICO TERRITORY

NEUTRAL STRIP

INDIAN TERRITORY

TEXAS

Note On 18th February, 1861, when the treaty was signed, the Western part of Kansas had not yet been transferred to Colorado Territory

This treaty promised that Black Kettle and his people would be protected by the US Government. The Southern Cheyenne, with Black Kettle, left for Sand Creek Reservation in south east Colorado. It was a poor reservation as there were no buffalo to hunt and the land was unworkable for food particularly.

But in order to keep his people safe, Black Kettle was given an American flag and a white flag by the Indian agent at the reservation to display on his tipi. The flag of peace and the flag of the white man. Black Kettle accepted both flags in good faith.

Public Domain Image

But other attacks were still occurring as the Cheyenne fought for their land and the need for supplies. By 1864 Colorado Governor John Evans was certain that he knew that Black Kettle had instigated these attacks. Which he hadn't.

Public Domain Image

85

John Evans, then made the decision to order all 'Friendly Indians of the Plains' to report to military posts or they would be assumed as 'hostiles'.

With authorisation from the War Department, a Colonel John M. Chivington led 3rd Colorado Cavalry of the '100-daysers' (its nickname came from the lack of battle experience required of the volunteers signing up for 100 days), just to fight the Cheyenne and Arapaho.

Colonel Chivington was an ambitious man and agreed with Governor Evans that they needed to utilise the time they had with the 3rd Colorado Cavalry and his '100 daysers' and do something radical about the 'Indian' problem quickly. And they only had 100 days to do it.

With this in mind, on 29th November, 1864, Chivington attacked Black Kettle's Sand Creek Reservation. Most of Black Kettle's warriors were out hunting, but this didn't stop the cavalry from killing and mutilating hundreds of Native Americans, mostly women and children, and burning down the camp itself.

The two flags, although displayed in good faith on Black Kettle's tipi as he had been advised to do, were totally ignored by Chivington and his men. This was then known as the Sand Creek Massacre and is also referred to as the Chivington Massacre.

Stone Rabbit
https://commons.wikimedia.org/wiki/File:Black_Kettle_at_Sand_Creek.jpg
https://creativecommons.org/licenses/by-sa/4.0/legalcode

Black Kettle managed to escape but had to return to try and save his wife who had been very badly injured. Despite this massacre Black Kettle continued to try and keep the peace between his people and the white man. Many Southern Cheyenne disagreed with him and joined forces with the Kiowa and Comanche and continued fighting the US Army and white settlers at every opportunity.

Black Kettle said *"Although wrongs have been done me, I live in hopes. I have not got two hearts.... I once thought that I was the only man that persevered to be the friend of the white man, but since they have come and cleaned out our lodges, horses, and everything else, it is hard for me to believe white men anymore."*

His wish for peace continued when he signed one of two treaties called the Little Arkansas Treaty between the 14th-18th October, 1865 which should have included reservations to be created and also where the US promised 'perpetual peace' to make amends for the Sand Creek Massacre. None of this sadly happened.

But in actual fact it just meant that the Cheyenne were, yet again, moved on to other lands in Oklahoma this time. This did not stop the warfare.

Black Kettle died during another US military attack on his camp on 27th November, 1868 as he and his people tried to flee from the troops of the 7th Cavalry attacking the camp and were killed trying to cross the Washita River to safety. This is now known as the Battle of Washita River and happened almost four years after the Sand Creek Massacre.

FETTERMAN AND THE BOZEMAN TRAIL

During Red Cloud's War, a name the US Army gave to the many conflicts between the US Army and the allied Northern Cheyenne, Lakota and Arapaho, one of the biggest recorded fights involving Red Cloud was the Fetterman Fight in 1866. This was also known as the Fetterman Massacre, the Battle of the Hundred in the Hands or Battle of Hundred Slain.

Captain William J. Fetterman, and Captain Frederick Brown, were sent from Fort Phil Kearny with 79 cavalry and infantrymen plus two civilians, to disperse a small war party that had attacked white men a few days earlier.

They disobeyed their orders thinking the mission a simple one, and they gave chase to a very small band of warriors, one of whom seemed injured. But this badly injured warrior was a decoy, and his name was Crazy Horse.

Public Domain Image
Crazy Horse

Fetterman, who was totally confident he would win this fight, followed the injured warrior with his soldiers and they were very cleverly ambushed by more than 2,000 Lakota, Cheyenne and Arapaho warriors. Fetterman and his troops lost their lives.

This Fetterman Massacre (or Fetterman Fight) gave the US Government food for thought and they decided to re-think their tactics and try to find peace with the various tribes. They understood that the various tribes had

had their lands and resources depleted by the constant arrival of the white man, and it was decided that perhaps lands should be designated for their sole use and not therefore encroached upon.

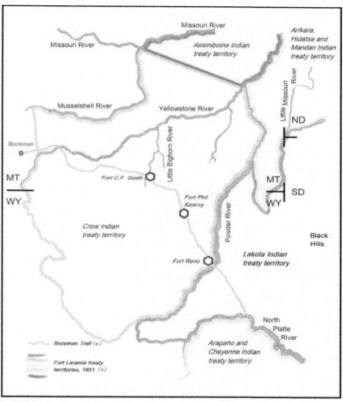

Naawada2016
https://commons.wikimedia.org/wiki/File:Bozeman_Trail,_the_forts_and_
the_Indian_territories.jpg
https://creativecommons.org/licenses/by-sa/4.0/legalcode

The US Government had already established many forts along what was known as the Bozeman Trail which connected to the Oregon Trail. Both trails allowed easy passage for the white settlers, immigrants and miners through the territory and straight through the buffalo feeding grounds. Red Cloud, along with the Lakota and the Cheyenne, battled with these white settlers and miners. The battles cut off food supplies to the white settlers and many times Fort Phil Kearny was attacked. Attacks and battles that continued for over two years.

This re-think on the US Government's part saw the birth of yet another treaty. The Fort Laramie Treaty of 1868 with the Lakota, Northern Cheyenne, Arapaho and other bands of tribes. The US Government agreed that they would abandon their forts, close the Bozeman Trail and withdraw completely from Lakota territory. The US Government also gave the Lakota Sioux possession of what is now the western half of South Dakota, along with large parts of Wyoming and Montana. Called The Great Sioux Reservation. On the strength of this, Red Cloud agreed to stop fighting. Peace at last?

Perhaps for a time.

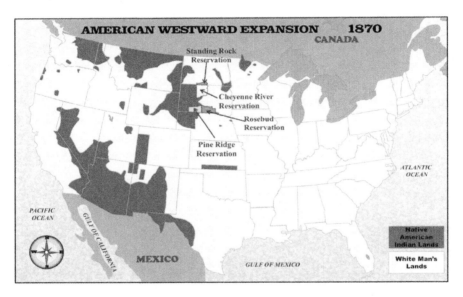

THE BLACK HILLS EXPEDITION AND THE LAST STAND

Around this time George Armstrong Custer was heading, unbeknown to him, to his 'last stand' when he led the *Black Hills Expedition.*

The *Black Hills Expedition* headed out on 2nd July, 1874 led by Lieutenant Colonel George Armstrong Custer from Fort Abraham Lincoln in the Dakota Territory. They were looking for sites to build more forts and the search for any gold too. And the Black Hills provided an abundance of gold.

In the 1868 treaty, signed at Fort Laramie, the US Government appeared to understand that the Sioux land in and around the Black Hills of Dakota was sacred, allocated it to the Sioux, and promised it would be 'off limits' to any white settlers, and that the Black Hills were now a part of the Great Sioux Reservation, just for the Sioux.

Public Domain Image

Custer

91

Until Custer's expedition found the gold that is, and the word of its find spread like wild fire. This was going to be the salvation needed to restore the US finances after the huge slump that followed the Panic of 1873. The land was now sacred to the US Government.

Eager gold diggers homed in on the area and the Fort Laramie Treaty of 1868 with the Sioux was reneged. This land that was sacred to the Sioux and was promised as a no-go area for any white settlers, was now sacred to the white man.

Public Domain Image

It was a dangerous life though with the constant Sioux attacks on the miners there, and the miners demanded protection from the US Army. And they got it. The army was ordered to move the Sioux away in any way that they could to secure the land. Tensions between the US Government and the Sioux were very high.

Reneging on yet another treaty the US Government turned the tables and made the peace talks into a demand that the Sioux left the area by 31st January, 1876, and join the reservation or they would be classed as enemies and be dealt with accordingly. Sitting Bull, as far as the US Government was concerned, was stopping their plans for expansion into Native American lands. Something had to be done about him and his people. And quickly.

Sitting Bull believed that the reservations were like being in prison and he did not want to be *'shut up in a corral'*. So let battle commence.

Sitting Bull was determined and instead of surrendering, he recruited a force of Native Americans including Arapaho, Cheyenne and the Sioux and they fought against General George Crook at Rosebud River in Montana where Sitting Bull's warriors had forced the army into a resounding retreat and won the Battle of the Rosebud on 17th June, 1876. Then he moved his warriors into the valley known as the Little Big Horn after victory celebrations.

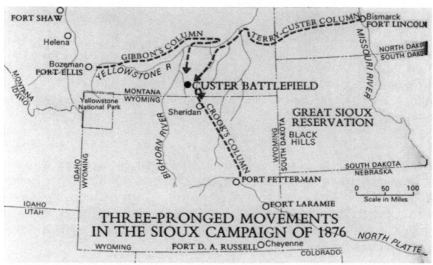

Public Domain Image

It was here that Sitting Bull performed the Sun Dance and the subsequent vision of *'soldiers falling into the camp like grasshoppers'* inspired his well established, and large numbers of warriors, to fight.

Public Domain Image

Then the 26th June, 1876 arrived and Custer, who was rather keen to prove himself, was not prepared to wait until General Alfred H. Terry, and Colonel John Gibbon had arrived with their troops, and decided to just to attack the Sioux camp.

But he hadn't realised how massive the camp was at Little Big Horn (also known as Greasy Grass River to the Lakota), with all the tribes from the reservations now lodging there in support of Sitting Bull and Crazy Horse. But that didn't deter Custer and he attacked the camp sending a battalion of men under Captain Frederick W. Benteen to scout south while Major Marcus A. Reno and 175 men advanced across the Little Bighorn River to face the enemy.

The battle was massive and the army's losses were massive too. The Native Americans were relentless in their quest for victory and their tactics, fighting skills and determination were just too much for the soldiers.

With the might of the Hunkpapa Sioux, Cheyenne, Miniconjou, Sans Arc, Oglala, a few Blackfoot and Brulee working together, the fight was on.

And fight they did, all extremely bravely under the circumstances much being hand to hand combat. You cannot take away the bravery of both sides in a battle such as this. Hand to hand combat, shooting at close range, fighting for your life, fending off tomahawks, trying to strike the enemy first. Trying to see through all the dust and smoke and hearing and fearing the whooping and yelling of the tribal battle cries as they got closer and closer. This was now the battle. The last stand.

Military horses, scared by the confusion, bolted in every direction and some were stopped by the Native American women from the camp. As luck would have it the horses were still carrying their saddlebags which produced further ammunition for the tribe to use along with the abandoned rifles lying next to their now dead or injured soldiers.

But it wasn't just the horses that ran, some of the soldiers had given up any attempt to keep a battle formation going and scattered. This made them very easy to pick off, and the warriors did just that.

Some soldiers managed to get to the river on their horses but the current in the river was too strong for them and many perished along with their horses. Others succeeded in heading up the hill to what they hoped would be safety. While others, less fortunate, were finished off by the women and young braves and their possessions claimed. Many were mutilated, as was the way for either the tribes or the white man. Both did terrible things to each other in the name of war.

Public Domain Image

95

Custer's 7th Cavalry had fought valiantly but were totally outnumbered. Custer had only succeeded in driving the tribes' bloodlust up after his surprise attack. The tribes' counter attack against the cavalry, surrounding them and killing all 209 of his troops, had not been how Custer had thought it would work out I am sure. Custer just didn't stand a chance.

This was literally Custer's last stand.

Public Domain Image
General Custer

Many claimed to have killed him too. No one really knows who did.

Four miles away, Major Reno and Captain Benteen had their own battle to fight as they encountered braves returning from the 'last stand' fight. At this stage the soldiers had only heard the noise of battle in the distance and were unaware that Custer had fallen. They defended where they were and fought for their lives too.

This battle continued with many more deaths and casualties. Sitting Bull, watching the proceedings from above, tried to call a halt to the battle by saying *"Let them go now, so some can go home and spread the news."*

The battle had fulfilled Sitting Bull's sun dance vision as soldiers had fallen into their camp and died. As the tribe celebrated with a victory dance, Sitting Bull was more reflective on the events and said, *"I feel sorry that too many were killed on each side, but when Indians must fight they must."*

The battle was considered as one of the greatest victories for the Native Americans against the US Army, but a stunning defeat for the US.

But who was to blame? The US Government needed someone to blame for this disaster. Was it Custer, Reno or Benteen? Or perhaps even President Ulysses S. Grant? It certainly was a bad judgement call as none of them thought for one minute that the 'Indians' would have such impressive battle tactics.

Regardless of all this the American public were still outraged over this huge defeat.

Because of the outrage, the victory for Sitting Bull was short-lived as the US Government sent in more and more troops into South Dakota over the next year to pursue the Sioux and to avenge the death of Custer and his men.

QUANAH PARKER – LAST CHIEF OF THE COMANCHE

The Comanche had also had a very difficult time trying to survive on their lands. The buffalo, their main food and resource, had been decimated by the buffalo hunters and the US Army had started a new tactic to get them off the land and onto a reservation.

The tactic was to hit them where it hurt. Their supplies, their clothing, their horses, their wealth, their homes. And it worked. Quanah Parker held out as long as he could. He and his people led the US Army a merry dance as they tried to catch him and end the constant battles. But it wasn't the endless battles that stopped Quanah Parker. It was that his people were starving and dying from the cold. He had to do something and surrender seemed like the only option now. And he did to Colonel Ranald S. Mackenzie.

Public Domain Image

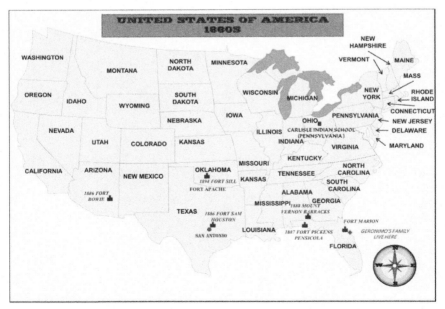

Public Domain Image

By 1875 they were on the Fort Sill reservation, along with many other tribes. But Quanah assimilated into the white man's world and became famous for turning the Comanche life around. He learnt how to live as a white man, became a business man, a cattle breeder, trading cattle, he built schools for the children, gained the friendship of President Roosevelt, leased the Comanche land to the cattle drives making money and a better life for himself and his people.

'Quanah Parker – One Man Two Worlds' is my book and talk on this great man and part of my *Native American Series*. An amazing man and warrior.

SITTING BULL

Sitting Bull and his people, the Sioux, had also been forced out of their lands and had fled for Canada in 1877 where they remained until 1881.

Public Domain Image

They were greeted warmly but their numbers grew rapidly, as word got out that a new life was possible in the 'Grandmother's Country' as the Sioux called Canada.

Lack of food and harsh winters led to Sitting Bull's surrendering on 20th July, 1881 at Fort Randall before he and his people were moved to the Standing Rock Reservation

In June 1885 he soon became a popular attraction in Buffalo Bill's Wild West Shows drawing crowds from everywhere just to come and see this 'savage' face to face. Sitting Bull signed on for an alledged signing bonus of $125 and $50 a week. Not bad for a 'savage'.

But he gave away a lot of his earnings, and the money he made for signing his signature or posing for photographs, to the homeless people or the beggars on the streets in the cities he visited. He could not understand how there was so much poverty amongst all the wealth in the US.

VICTORIO

Victorio was born in 1825, was a warrior and chief of the Warm Springs band of the Chihenne of the Apache tribe.

In his twenties, he fought alongside Mangas Coloradas, the principal leader of the whole Tchihendeh Apache division (who took him as his son-in-law). Mangas Coloradas mentored not only Victorio, but also Geronimo and Cochise in ambush and defensive battle tactics, of fortifying your stronghold, keeping rough country to the rear, and fighting from high ground. Utilising the terrain by using nature's weapons in the rocks by using the rocks and nature itself as ammunition, setting off rock slides, and

Public Domain Image

knowing that the US soldiers couldn't fight successfully on this ground. Victorio was then saving bullets for bigger battles.

The Apache also found that the soldiers, although trying to catch them, were unable to keep up the pace that they had. The Apache were used to travelling great distances without breaks to rest, whereas the soldiers often stopped for rest and refreshments.

By 1877, Victorio and his followers had already been forced onto the San Carlos Reservation in Arizona Territory. But Victorio and his followers were very unhappy with the conditions as they were unacceptable for his people due to the 110 degree temperatures there.

Because of the conditions Victorio and his people left the reservation twice, seeking and temporarily obtaining hospitality in Fort Stanton or the Warm Springs Reservation (Ojo Calente). Here they were among their Sierra Blanca and Sacramento Mescalero allies and relatives and were content living there. But the US Government now classed them as outlaws or renegades.

In the October of 1878 Victorio was told to bring himself and his people back to the San Carlos reservation by the US Government. This was not something Victorio wanted to do and he and his followers literally ran for the hills.

In what is now known as Victorio's War, from September 1879 to October 1880, Victorio led a band of Apaches, of around 200 warriors, in battles with the US and Mexican armies and the settlers of New Mexico, Texas, and northern Mexico. With the battles re-started, Victorio had the ideal fighting partner in a man called Chief Nana who, in 1879, was a 70 year old warrior. He was a lower chief than Victorio, but still happy to be part of Victorio's raids and proved himself to be a formidable warrior and asset to Victorio. Chief Nana reportedly said *"It is not too late so long as one Apache lives"*.

With the combined effort of the US Army and the Mexican Army, they were able to track down Victorio and his band of Apache in the Tres Castillo Mountains. Having sent Nana and Mangus (son of Mangas Coloradas) to raid for food and ammunition, Victorio, with only a few warriors and even less ammunition to fight back, he and his few warriors were surrounded by 260 men from the Mexican Army under Colonel Joaquin Terrazas in the Battle of Tres Castillos.

The battle ended Victorio's War.

Victorio was reported to have been killed by a scout during the battle, whereas the Apache say that he committed suicide rather than face capture. He was 55 years old. The end of another era.

"He died as he had lived free and inconquerable."

GERONIMO AND NANA

Only Geronimo and Nana now remained and Geronimo was pursued relentlessly with the new ruling of 'Hot Pursuit' which meant the US Army could cross into any border to capture him and his people.

Public Domain Image

Public Domain Image

Geronimo knew change was coming. He could feel it and see it as his tribe's numbers reduced so badly and supplies became harder and harder to accumulate. He had already had surrender talks with General Howard but that didn't happen. He did not trust his words.

But on 4th September, 1886, he too surrendered to General Nelson A. Miles handing over his rifle to him and becoming a prisoner of war along with his people. Separated from their families they lived in various prison camps.

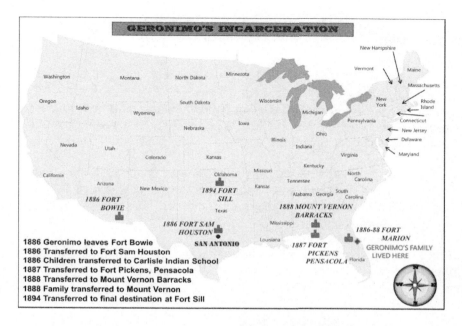

In 1886 in Fort Sam Houston, in 1887 Fort Pickens, Pensacola, 1888 Mount Vernon Barracks near Alabama before being allowed to settle on the reservation at Fort Sill Oklahoma in 1894, re-joining their families there. Nana died here on 19th May, 1896.

In 1898 Geronimo became a celebrity appearing in various shows. The two largest were the Pan-American Exposition at Buffalo, New York, in 1901, and the St. Louis World's Fair in 1904. Under Army guard, Geronimo dressed in traditional clothing and posed for photographs and sold the buttons from his shirt. Then bought more, had them sewn on, and sold them again.

In February 1909 Geronimo was thrown from his horse and not found until much later but pneumonia had set in and he died on 17th February, 1909. His last words were reported to be said to his nephew, *"I should have never surrendered. I should have fought until I was the last man alive."*

GHOST DANCE AND SITTING BULL

While Buffalo Bill was touring Europe and taking time out to meet with Pope Leo XIII in 1890, things had taken a turn for the worst for his show stopper Sitting Bull.

As far as the Indian Agent McLaughlin was concerned the 'trouble maker', Sitting Bull, had sadly returned to the reservation at Standing Rock as his time with the show had ended. He was not best pleased having Sitting Bull back.

And now the Ghost Dance had started to take effect within the tribes of the Sioux on various other reservations. This was not good news for any of the Indian Agents on reservations.

The Ghost Dance arrived at a time on the reservation when the Native Americans were suffering great hardship due to the very harsh winters, lack of food, and lack of meaning in their lives as their traditions had been taken away from them. Their sense of freedom and their love of life on their land had gone.

Word of the Ghost Dance had already reached Pine Ridge, Rosebud and Cheyenne River Reservations and the Native Americans there were ready for some form of spiritual guidance to get them out of their situation with the white man. This new religion gave them hope, something to live for.

It was basically a vision that a Paiute Indian named Wovoka (also known as prophet Jack Wilson), proclaimed that Jesus Christ had returned to Earth in the form of an Native American, and news of this vision had spread like wild fire amongst the Plains Indians culminating on the reservations themselves.

If the 'Ghost Dance' was performed, then the 'Indians would live forever in a land that was free of the white man, full of different game for them to hunt, no sickness or hunger, peace at last, and all their generations of ancestors would be there waiting for them.'

Sitting Bull was not convinced.

The Ghost Dance Movement as it was called required the tribes to dance and chant to help their deceased relatives rise from the dead, and herald the return of the buffalo. And the dance was performed slow and solemn as a shuffle in silence to a slow, single drumbeat. A dancing ceremony, that would rid the Native American land of white people, so that Native Americans could establish themselves back into their traditions and way of life again. It would be like a dream come true for them. 'A Man Called Sitting Bull'

Public Domain Image

The dance also required the wearing of shirts that had magical powers and would stop any of the white man's bullets from penetrating and harming the wearer. Or so they believed.

Because of the unrest that had been caused in the other reservations by the Ghost Dance, soldiers had arrived and were literally on 'stand by' just in-case they were needed. They did not feel that they should just steam in and put a stop to it but hoped that their presence might just halt things.

Newspapers had already reported of this terrible 'savage' dance and that the crazed new religion was stirring the Sioux into a dangerous frenzy. At Standing Rock, McLaughlin had already decided that Sitting Bull would incite his people to revolt and his opinion in this respect just made the situation worse. He was a worried man and to solve the problem, he ordered Sitting Bull to be arrested.

The Indian Police were sent to Sitting Bull's camp to arrest him. This was on 15th December, 1890 and it turned out to be not only a day long remembered, but as a very bad day for many. The Sioux particularly. As just before dawn, 39 police officers made up of Lakota Sioux themselves, and four volunteers (Special Constables sworn in for this task wearing white handkerchiefs around their necks to distinguish them from the others), arrived and surrounded Sitting Bull's cabin. Then they barged in.

Bullhead, the leader of the police, told Sitting Bull that the Indian agent needed to speak with him and he needed to come with them. He assured Sitting Bull that once the meeting was over he could return to his cabin and family.

Sitting Bull refused, and the Indian Police tried to force him. This angered the tribal members congregating outside the cabin, and they gathered to protect him. Sitting Bull stood firm, and a scuffle started.

During the scuffle, Catch-the-Bear, a Lakota Sioux, aimed his rifle and shot Bullhead in his side, who reacted badly as he fell by shooting Sitting Bull in the chest with his revolver. Another police officer, Red Tomahawk, reacted really badly too by shooting Sitting Bull in the back of the head, and Sitting Bull dropped to the ground. The great spiritual leader Sitting Bull died immediately on 15th December, 1890.

This started a vicious battle as furious Sioux attacked the Indian Police with guns, knives and clubs.

Sitting Bull being killed this way infuriated the tribe and the fight continued with several men losing their lives. The Sioux killed six of the policemen on the spot, but two others died shortly afterwards. Bullhead included after many more bullets were shot into his body.

Sitting Bull's death led many of the Sioux to leave the reservation rather quickly to save any further deaths, particularly theirs, from revenge or retribution from the soldiers there.

Public Domain Image

Two weeks later the massacre at Wounded Knee would take place.

WOUNDED KNEE MASSACRE

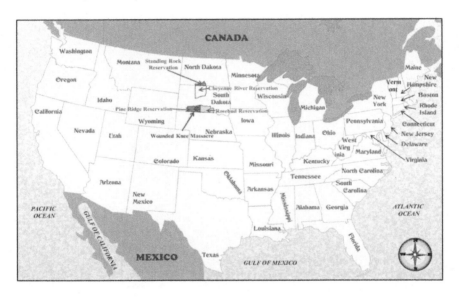

The massacre of several hundred Sioux has now become famous in history as the *Wounded Knee Massacre* or the *Battle of Wounded Knee.*

It happened about two weeks after Sitting Bull's death on 29th December, 1890 near Wounded Knee Creek on the Lakota Pine Ridge Indian Reservation, South Dakota.

A troop of the US 7th Cavalry led by Major Samuel M. Whitside stopped Spotted Elk's band of Miniconjou and thirty eight Hunkpapa Lakota near Porcupine Butte, as they were trying to escape from the reservation after Sitting Bull's death fearing repercussions. The US 7th Cavalry escorted them to Wounded Knee Creek, about five miles further on, and they were advised to make camp there.

The rest of the cavalry, led by Colonel James W. Forsyth, arrived and surrounded the whole of the camp. They had brought four Hotchkiss mountain guns with them.

Public Domain Image

On the morning of 29th December, the US Cavalry troops entered the camp with the aim of disarming the tribes and it went very badly wrong.

Several variations on the same theme have been recorded on how the events of the massacre occurred. One of the most written about versions states that a US Cavalry soldier tried to disarm a deaf tribesman called Black Coyote, who for obvious reasons, did not understand why the soldier was trying to take his rifle. The rifle had cost him a lot, and he didn't want to just hand it over to a stranger. Sadly in the scuffle, it went off accidentally and further shooting commenced.

It all happened so quickly, and at close range, that many warriors were killed or wounded before they had a chance to retaliate. Some managed to re-claim their rifles and fire back but as they had nowhere to hide and gain any cover; they were picked off quickly.

The soldiers brought in the Hotchkiss guns and managed to decimate the tipis and the occupants with their deadly fire. Admittedly with it being such close range, quite a few soldiers lost their lives to 'friendly fire'.

Some of the women and children managed to flee the camp and hide from the shooting, but there was only blood lust now and the soldiers decided to spread out and finish off any wounded tribesmen or women and children that they found.

Public Domain Image

More soldiers used horses to pursue some of the fleeing women and children, quite often for miles just to make sure that no one escaped.

When the shooting had stopped over, *"250 men, women, and children of the Lakota had been killed and 51 were wounded (4 men and 47 women and children, some of whom died later); some estimates placed the number of dead as high as 300."*

Three days later, after a very bad blizzard, the military hired civilians to deal with the dead at Wounded Knee.

Public Domain Image

Public Domain Image

Remains of Spotted Elk

What they found would live with them forever as the dead had frozen where they had died.

Once they had gathered the frozen bodies, they were interred in a mass grave on a hill overlooking where the camp had been, and exactly on the spot from where the Hotchkiss guns had been placed to fire on the Sioux.

History states that four infants were found alive amongst the dead. What happened to them I cannot tell you.

Public Domain Image

Although the number of Native Americans that were killed here is unknown as the Sioux removed some of the dead later, the mass grave held 84 men, 44 women and 18 children.

This massacre ended the Ghost Dance Movement.

MANIFEST DESTINY

Public Domain Image

MANIFEST DESTINY

Now that all the Native American tribes were living on various reservations on very small parcels of land, the American expansion and Manifest Destiny was complete. Thousands had arrived and this huge influx of eager settlers had helped to fulfil America's 'Manifest Destiny' to *'become a continental nation'*.

Public Domain Image

Manifest Destiny was a phrase used in 1845, and was explained as *'the idea that the United States is destined—by God, its advocates believed—to expand its dominion and spread democracy and capitalism across the entire North American continent.'* Wikipedia

'And to the Americans, Manifest Destiny was the belief that it was settlers' God-given duty and right to settle the North American continent. This proved successful and 'in 1893 historian Frederick Jackson Turner declared the frontier closed, citing the 1890 census as evidence, and with that, the period of westward expansion ended.' Wikipedia

America was now a huge nation.

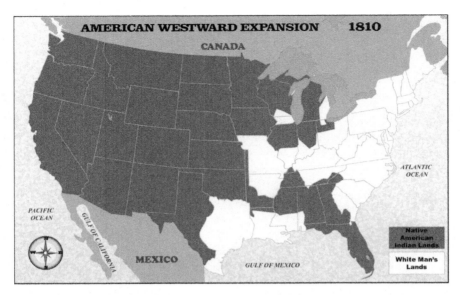

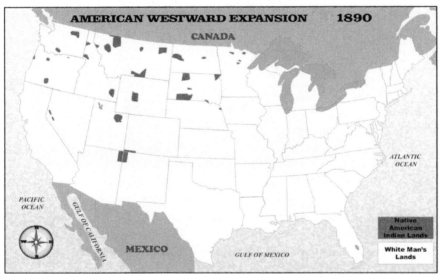

THE LEGENDS

Public Domain Image

LAWLESSNESS

Lawlessness started to creep into many of the boomtowns. Law enforcement was attempted by many usually creating a role rather quickly for a new sheriff or Marshall in town when he either left quickly or found a permanent spot in 'Boot Hill'.

In San Francisco, in order to try and combat lawlessness, the San Francisco Committee of Vigilance was formed. They were a vigilante group trying to stem the crime and corruption in San Francisco, and became the instigators of the drumhead trials and death sentences to those well known offenders. They authorised lynchings, whippings and deportation. All because of the thousands that had arrived seeking their fortune in gold and the problems that were created alongside this.

Other settlements created their own ways of trying to enforce the law of their land, but a lot of the time it was mainly concerned, responsible citizens who just wanted to keep the peace. They had their homes, their gold mining stakes, their businesses to protect as well as their families. There was a lot at stake.

HANGING OF WHITTAKER AND MCKENZIE,
By the San Francisco Vigilance Committee.
Public Domain Image

It has been known that some vigilante groups, once they had caught the perpetrators, would deal with them severely and punish without any form of trial, and usually shot or hung those perpetrators.

But sometimes the risk of being caught and dealt with severely was a risk worth taking. That's why we have legends.

BILLY THE KID

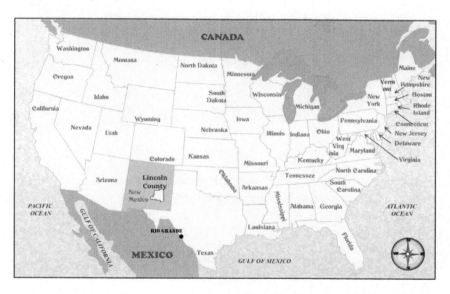

       While Little Big Horn was being fought and won by the Native American, and Custer was no more, another well known name started to make his mark in the annuls of American history. Henry McCarty, or as we know him, Billy the Kid.

Henry McCarty was born in 1859, and much later worked as a 'cowhand' for a time on the ranch of John Henry Tunstall near the Rio Grande in Lincoln County.

Prior to this Henry McCarty, also known as William H. Bonney and later Billy the Kid, had already started on his way of building a reputation for himself. At the age of 16 years he was arrested for stealing food, then a few days later he robbed a Chinese laundry and was arrested again. But he somehow managed to escape and headed to Arizona Territory. Now he was a fugitive and an outlaw.

In 1876 McCarty managed to gain a role as cook in the Hotel de Luna, and later as a ranch hand on the ranch of Henry Hooker who was well known in the area. During his time on the ranch McCarty met John R. Mackie who was a Scottish born criminal and formerly a US Cavalry private. Mackie showed McCarty that there were easier ways of making a living. And Camp Grant became a target for the two of them as they stole horses from the soldiers and McCarty earned the name of 'Kid Antrim' because of his youthful appearance and Antrim was believed to be his step-father's surname.

Public Domain Image

Camp Grant

After escaping from Camp Grant where he was arrested for stealing horses, McCarty's stay in Arizona was shortlived as he killed his first man, a blacksmith, in August 1877 after an argument. The blacksmith, Francis P. 'Windy' Cahill and McCarty got into a tussle, a gun was involved and McCarty was quicker gaining the gun and Cahill was mortally wounded.

He headed back to New Mexico where he had originally come from. While he was there he joined a group of cattle rustlers, called 'The Boys', raiding the herds of John Chisum in Lincoln County. His notoriety was mentioned in the local newspapers and this is when he took on the name of William H. Bonney.

After a falling out with 'The Boys' he started working for Mr. Tunstall on his ranch in 1878, and Bonney became part of the Lincoln County War. Mr. Tunstall had a business opponent named Lawrence Murphy. Murphy seemed to have his 'fingers in many pies' and owned the bulk of Lincoln County.

Public Domain Image
Tunstall

Public Domain Image
Lawrence Murphy

Public Domain Image
Lincoln County Sheriff William J. Brady

Alexander McSween was a young lawyer and business partner of Tunstall. He owed money to Murphy's business partner Dolan, and Dolan called in the debt.

Dolan gained a court order and asked Lincoln County Sheriff William J. Brady to claim Tunstall's cattle to cover the debt.

Sheriff Brady formed a posse to reclaim the cattle from Tunstall, and Tunstall heard that Brady was on his way and tried to intervene. Sadly one of the posse shot and killed Tunstall while another made sure by shooting him in the head. This was the start of the Lincoln County War.

Dick Brewer

Dick Brewer, who was a cattle foreman for Tunstall, and William Bonney formed a posse themselves after Tunstall's murder. Brewer and Bonney swore affidavits against Brady and his posse, and obtained murder warrants from Lincoln County justice of the peace John B. Wilson. Bonney's posse was deputised to serve the arrest warrants on his killers, with Brewer chosen to lead the posse. The Regulators originated from that posse. Tunstall's ranch-hands and other local citizens formed this group to avenge Tunstall's murder, and stop what they believed as the 'corrupt territorial criminal justice system' that Murphy, Dolan and his friends controlled.

The Regulators managed to capture William Morton and Frank Baker, both who were accused of killing Tunstall. They were killed while apparently 'trying to escape'.

On 1st April the Regulators ambushed Sheriff Brady and his deputies and during the battle Brady was killed as was Sheriff Hindman. Dick Brewer died there too. Bonney and two of the Regulators were charged with the murder of Lincoln County Sheriff William J. Brady and one of his deputies. Although indicted for the murder of Brady, Billy the Kid seems to have appeared and is now ready to take part in a battle at McSween's home.

Possibly hiding, pure speculation here, with the Regulators at the McSween home, the home was attacked by Murphy supporters. The house was set on fire and shooting ensued and in the confusion McSween was killed. Billy the Kid then shot the man (Robert W. Beckwith) who had shot McSween. And escaped again.

Events took a bit of a turn around when on 5th October, 1878, US Marshal John Sherman informed newly appointed Territorial Governor and former Union Army General Lew Wallace that he had warrants for the arrest of Billy the Kid, but was unable to put them into force *"owing to the disturbed condition of affairs in that county, resulting from the acts of a desperate class of men."*

Wallace issued an amnesty proclamation on 13th November, 1878, pardoning anyone who was involved in Tunstall's murder. Unless they had been indicted for murder that is, which meant that Billy the Kid was definitely excluded.

Public Domain Image

Tom O'Folliard

But an incident occurred that almost solved this amnesty problem for Billy the Kid when he and Tom O'Folliard witnessed Huston Chapman, an attorney in Lincoln County, set on fire after he had been shot. Witnesses agreed that Billy the Kid and O'Folliard had nothing to do with this murder as they had been held at gunpoint themselves by Jesse Evans and told to watch. Billy the Kid wrote to Governor Wallace offering information regarding this murder in exchange for his own amnesty.

Governor Wallace agreed and asked for a secret meeting to discuss this promising him protection and amnesty if he did testify.

On 20th March, Wallace wrote to Billy the Kid saying *"to remove all suspicion of understanding, I think it better to put the arresting party in charge of Sheriff Kimball who shall be instructed to see that no violence is used."* Billy the Kid agreed to this.

On 21st March, Billy the Kid and Tom O'Folliard allowed themselves to be arrested by Sheriff George Kimball's posse and brought back to Lincoln County. Billy the Kid gave his statement as promised and did testify in court.

And this is when things started to change. He was not set free afterwards as promised. Months later he was still held in custody. This was not what was agreed with the Governor. Billy the Kid could not see his amnesty coming anytime soon, so he escaped from Lincoln County jail on 17th June, 1879.

Life continued for Billy the Kid and a new friendship was formed with a rancher called Jim Greathouse. This led to Billy the Kid meeting a man called Dave Rudabaugh, the man Wyatt Earp was so keen to arrest in later years.

Returning to Greathouse's ranch rather quickly, as they were being chased by a posse, it wasn't long before they were surrounded. Billy the Kid told the posse that they had Greathouse as a hostage and at this point the deputy sheriff, James Carlyle, offered himself in exchange. This was accepted and Greathouse, Billy's friend, was released safely.

But Carlyle tried to escape by jumping through one of the windows and was shot and killed by his own men. Further shooting occurred until the posse left giving Billy the Kid, Rudabaugh and Wilson the chance to escape themselves.

Billy the Kid wrote to Governor Wallace to plead his innocence in the Carlyle shooting but this did no good.

He was on the run again and it was not long after this Billy was to meet his match in the shape of Sheriff Pat Garrett.

Public Domain Image
Pat Garrett

By 13th December, 1880, there was a bounty on Billy the Kid's head of $500 and Pat Garrett seemed to be the best man to capture him. And he did with his posse on 23rd December, 1880. Tom O'Folliard was killed during this capture.

Billy the Kid, Dave Rudabaugh and the others were shackled and taken by train to Fort Sumner, Santa Fe, then New Mexico. It was a rough ride as angry mobs were waiting at each stop and they wanted blood. Billy's blood. It took a lot of effort from Garrett to keep his prisoners safe.

Billy the Kid spent time writing to Governor Wallace trying to find clemency but failed. In April 1881 Billy the Kid went on trial for the murder of Sheriff Brady and was found guilty of first degree murder. He was sentenced to hang on 13th May.

He was moved to Lincoln where he was to be hanged, and held there under guard in the town's courthouse. While Deputy Bob Ollinger took other prisoners across the street for a meal, Billy the Kid asked his guard, Deputy James Bell, if he could use the outhouse. He was taken there. Somehow Billy the Kid managed to escape from his handcuffs and when returning to the courthouse, beat Bell with the handcuffs, grabbed his revolver and shot Bell in the back as Bell tried to get away.

Billy the Kid broke into Garrett's office and stole a rifle left by Ollinger. Billy the Kid waited upstairs for his return which Ollinger did due to the noise of gunshot, only to find Billy the Kid upstairs and it is said that Billy the Kid said, "Look up old boy, and see what you get." Ollinger did look up and Billy the Kid shot him.

Garrett pursued Billy the Kid constantly after this and eventually heard rumours that Billy the Kid was in the home of Billy's friend, Pete Maxwell.

Historians have differing versions of the situation that followed. But the upshot was that on 14th July, 1881, Billy the Kid heard voices while he was at the Maxwell home and walking into a darkened room he is said to have said "Quien es? Quien es?" (Spanish for Who is it? Who is it?) Garrett recognised the voice in the dark, drew his revolver and shot Billy the Kid in the chest just above his heart. He shot a second time but missed apparently. Billy the Kid may have died instantly. We will never know.

Billy the Kid's body was examined and confirmed that it was him and certified as such. His death was classed a justifiable homicide. He was buried the next day, next to his friends Tom O'Folliard and Charlie Bowdre, and his grave was marked by a wooden marker.

Public Domain Image

Garrett travelled to claim the bounty but the Acting Governor refused to hand over the money. But the people of many cities raised over $1,300 to reward Garrett for killing the notorious Billy the Kid and eventually the original $500 was granted to him over a year later.

Garrett himself asked a friend, Marshall Upton, to help him write his story of Billy the Kid's death, as some felt that Garrett had killed him unfairly. The book is called *'The Authentic Life of Billy the Kid'* and was published in 1882 becoming an historical reference about Billy's life itself.

But was Billy the Kid dead? He had at one time been a friend of Garrett's so perhaps Garrett had staged the whole thing to help him escape again. Many have apparently claimed to be Billy the Kid and have been disproven too.

But one Texas man called Ollie P. Roberts (Brushy Bill Roberts) actually sought a pardon from the Governor of New Mexico in 1948 as Billy the Kid. It was refused but had an impact on the area. So much so that when he died shortly afterwards, a Billy the Kid museum was opened.

DNA samples have tried to be cross matched with that of his new claimants and so far nothing has been conclusive. Another mystery not yet solved even in this day and age. But it just makes the whole history of his life and death all the more fascinating.

Public Domain Image

PAT GARRETT

Patrick Floyd Jarvis Garrett was born in 1850 in Alabama. His family originated from England and migrated to America. Although Garrett was known as a bartender, an old western lawman, the sheriff of Lincoln County and Dona Ana County, New Mexico, his real claim to fame was the killing of Billy the Kid.

Losing both his parents within a year of each other, he and his siblings were taken on by relatives until Garrett was eighteen and he left Louisiana in 1869.

Although not a great deal is known about his life then, we do know that by 1876 he was a buffalo hunter in Texas and it was during this time that he killed his first man, another buffalo hunter, and he gave himself up for justice. They didn't prosecute and Garrett turned his horse in the direction of Fort Sumner, New Mexico, and found work as a cowhand with Pedro Menard 'Pete' Maxwell.

By 1880 Garrett was a married man with children, but it was also the year his association with Billy the Kid started.

Garrett had been elected sheriff of Lincoln County in November 1880 beating the existing sheriff George Kimball (or Kimbrell, both names are used). But Garrett's term of office wasn't due to start until 1881, and he became a deputy for Sheriff Kimball (or Kimbrell) in the meantime. This gave him the opportunity through his commission to pursue Billy the Kid over all the county area.

In December 1880, hearing that Billy the Kid and his gang of Charlie Bowdre, Tom Pickett, Billy Wilson and Tom O'Folliard, were heading for a nearby ranch at Fort Sumner, so did Garrett and his posse. Garrett's men thought that, during a gun battle on the way to the ranch, they had shot and killed the Kid but in fact it was O'Folliard they had killed instead. Billy and the others had escaped.

Public Domain Image
Charles Bowdre

Public Domain Image
Tom O'Folliard

But shortly after in a delightfully named place called Stinking Springs, Billy the Kid and the others were captured. Both Billy the Kid and Dave Rudabaugh had now gained celebrity status with the public. Mainly because they wanted to lynch them. Billy the Kid was sentenced to hang. It seemed like it was all over. Until Garrett left Lincoln County for White Oaks, possibly to buy lumber for the gallows. He left Bob Ollinger and James Bell in charge of Billy the Kid and warned them that he would probably try to escape. He was right.

Billy the Kid escaped killing the two deputies. The hunt was on yet again with a $500 reward to anyone who can capture him.

The following July 1881, Garrett returned to Fort Sumner and discovered that Billy the Kid was staying very close by with 'Pete' Maxwell. Garrett, John W. Poe, a cattle detective, and Tom 'Kip' McKinney, headed to Maxwell's ranch. And this is where Billy the Kid's story ended, in the dark with a bullet in the chest just above his heart.

Garrett tried to gain the reward money of $500 but, through a technicality, the Governor refused to pay. He headed to Las Vegas and discovered that the citizens in Dona Ana County had raised a reward for him instead with $1,300 and $600 from Santa Fe County. Much later he actually received the $500 reward initially promised.

Well you would have thought that would be the end of the story, but books and dime novels featured Billy the Kid as a hero. While Garrett was classed as a killer. This unwelcome attention drove Garrett to help write *'The Authentic Life of Billy the Kid'* as he needed his side of the story told.

Public Domain Image

One of many books about Billy the Kid

Garrett tried various alternative occupations as he did not seek re-election as sheriff of Lincoln County. He was even a lieutenant in the Texas Rangers for a short time.

Around 1885 he tried his hand at ranching and as a company man when he discovered a reservoir of artesian water in the Roswell area. *'Artesian water is apparently naturally filtered free flowing spring water that comes from wells deep underground. Pumps to gain the water are*

not necessary as the water moves up to the surface of its own accord due to pressure.' Wikipedia

With two other men he formed the 'Pecos Valley Irrigation and Investment Company'.

You can imagine a find such as this during this era would be quite enormous, but sadly no matter how he tried and the efforts he put into his irrigation schemes, his partners found a way to remove him.

By 1896 Garrett was again sheriff, this time in Dona Ana County, New Mexico, and he became involved in the disappearance of Colonel Albert Jennings Fountain and his eight year old son Henry, thought to have been assassinated. Nothing was ever found and even with the help of the Pinkertons, the mystery was not solved. But Garrett came to the rescue.

Over the next two years Garrett had gathered enough information on the disappearance to make arrests. His targets were Oliver M. Lee, William McNew, Bill Carr and James Gililland. He quickly found and arrested McNew and Carr. But not without a fight.

Lee and Gililland fought from the roof of their hide out, a deputy was wounded and Garrett was wounded too. Garrett, in order to try and save his deputy, asked for a truce with the fugitives and left with his injured deputy who sadly died on the road back.

Lee and Gililland escaped capture for quite a few months before they surrendered to Sheriff George Curry in 1898, but were found not guilty of all their crimes.

In 1899 Garrett killed for the last time; a fugitive from murder named Norman Newman. But his life took a hugely different turn when President Theodore Roosevelt nominated Garrett for the role of Collectors of Customs in El Paso and a 'White House Gunfighter' along with Bat Masterson and Ben Daniels. His role was confirmed by US Senate. But he wasn't everyone's choice and this caused some conflict.

In 1903 he was charged with disturbing the peace when he got into a fist fight with an employee. The complaints about Garrett landing on Roosevelt's desk were beginning to grow but Roosevelt still gave Garrett the benefit of the doubt.

Public Domain Image

Roosevelt's Rough Riders

But the final straw for Roosevelt was an invite he sent to Garrett to attend a Rough Riders reunion in April 1905.

Rough Riders were members of the 1st Volunteer Cavalry, in the Spanish-American War, recruited by Theodore Roosevelt and composed of cowhands, miners, law-enforcement officials, and college athletes.

Garrett had not been part of the Rough Riders and this caused some dissent around Washington. But Garrett attended and brought along a guest in the shape of a 'prominent Texas cattleman', Tom Powers. Roosevelt, Garrett and Powers posed for a few photos together to mark the occasion and it wasn't until later that Roosevelt was informed that Powers was not a 'prominent Texas cattleman' but the owner of a 'notorious dive' of a saloon in El Paso. That was the final straw and Garrett was replaced very quickly as Collector of Customs.

Things seemed to go downhill quickly for Garrett after that although he did not seem to change his ways to help or stop this. He was financially in a lot of debt and tried to gain a vacant role of Superintendent in a Santa Fe jail. But again while waiting for this role to begin, he got himself tied up with a prostitute and the role of Superintendent was withdrawn.

Goat herding was really the cause of Pat Garrett's death when his son, Dudley Poe Garrett, signed a lease for a ranch with a Jesse Wayne Brazel in 1908. Problem was, the ranch was set to be a goat ranch and objecting strongly, Pat Garrett tried to break the lease. This attempt was refused and it went to court.

Trying to solve the problem was a man named Miller, who acted as mediator between the two men over this issue. Brazel agreed to stop the lease if someone bought the goats. All 1,200 of them. This was agreed with, and Carl Adamson bought the goats. But still Brazel wasn't happy.

He thought that there were more goats than he had been paid for. The dispute continued.

Mblitch at en.wikipedia
https://commons.wikimedia.org/wiki/File:Garrett_Memorial.jpg
Garrett Memorial
https://creativecommons.org/licenses/by-sa/3.0/legalcode

Agreeing to meet to discuss this further, Garrett and Adamson rode out for the meeting and at some stage Brazel arrived and Garrett was shot and killed and his body left at the side of the road. But killed by whom?

Brazel surrendered himself as the killer to the sheriff in Las Cruces and was jailed. The only other witness was Adamson and it doesn't appear that he said much to change the day's events. Brazel is alleged to have said of Adamson, "He knows the whole thing and knows I shot in self-defence."

Brazel was held for trial which concluded in May 1909. Adamson never appeared at the trial, but Brazel was acquitted.

There is now an historical marker at the site of Garrett's death. Garrett was aged 57 years when he died and as he was too tall for a normal coffin, and one had to shipped from El Paso to hold his remains. He was buried on 5th March, 1908.

Public Domain Image

JESSE AND FRANK JAMES

By 1881, a man called Jesse James only had a year to live. He was a very young man and it wasn't that he was unwell. It was simply because of the life he had led. There was money on his head. He was a wanted man.

Jesse Woodson James was born 3rd April, 1847 and he was the leader of the James-Younger Gang well known for robbing trains, stagecoaches and banks. Before this he and his brother Alexander Franklin James, born 10th January, 1843, were part of the pro-Confederate guerrillas known as the 'bushwhackers' during the American Civil War.

'The American Civil War (April 1861-May 1865) was a war between the Union (the North against slavery), and the Confederacy (the South pro slavery). The reason for the war was slavery, especially as slavery had now expanded into territories acquired due to the Louisiana Purchase and the Mexican/American War.' Wikipedia

It wasn't just the American westward expansion that had created so much change over the land, but also there was a huge amount of changes going on North / South too. Changes still felt to this day.

Frank James had already been involved in attacks against Union sympathizers in the region. But in May 1863, a young Jesse James while at his family's farm, was ambushed and witnessed his stepfather being hung from a tree by Union militiamen seeking the whereabouts of Frank and his fellow rebels. Luckily his step father survived but it saw a change in Jesse.

Public Domain Image

William 'Bloody Bill' Anderson

Witnessing his step father being attacked led to Jesse, aged 16, to follow in Frank's footsteps and became a bushwhacker himself.

'He and his brother joined a gang led by William "Bloody Bill" Anderson and participated in a number of violent incidents, including a September 1864 raid on Centralia, Missouri. In that raid, at least 20 unarmed Union soldiers were forced from a train and executed by the guerrillas, who then slaughtered more than 100 federal troops trying to hunt them down. The guerrilla's viciously mutilated many of their victims' corpses.' Wikipedia

In May 1865, after Confederate General Robert E. Lee, had surrendered, Jesse was shot in the chest during a fight with Union troops near Lexington, Missouri. Luckily he was given care and attention from his cousin Zerelda "Zee" Mimms, his wife to be in 1875, and made a full recovery.

It wasn't long before he became notorious as the leader of the James-Younger gang continuing and increasing their efforts by robbing stagecoaches and trains. The James-Younger gang, was made up of Cole Younger and his brothers Jim and Bob, Clell Miller, Charlie Pitts, Bill Chadwell (known as Bill Stiles) and of course Frank and Jesse. They carried out a string of robberies.

One in particular had Frank and Jesse James, Cole and Jim Younger and nine other members targeting the Daviess County Savings Association in Gallatin, Missouri on 13th February, 1866. During this robbery Jesse shot and killed the bank cashier as he thought the man was Samuel Cox, the leader of the pro-Union militia and the man who had killed Bloody Bill Anderson. During this robbery a 17 year old boy was also killed.

Public Domain Image
John W. Sheets

Jesse thought that he had, at last, gained revenge for his leader's death. But he was mistaken, as the cashier had nothing to do with it. The cashiers name was John W. Sheets. Both Frank and Jesse later denied being anywhere near when the robbery occurred. But this robbery started the publicity label of 'outlaw' for Jesse James. There was now a reward of $3,000 for their capture.

A newspaper man John Newman Edwards, picked up their daring deeds and wrote about them in very exciting and highly embellished terms. But it sold newspapers and dime novels too.

And they gave many opportunities for more to be written about them as in Iowa they held up the treasurer's office and they robbed a bank stealing $10,000.

The Kansas City Fair in 1872 fared even less when they stole all the takings. Then they moved on to bigger fish in the shape of trains.

Their first was the Chicago Rock Island and Pacific train. Using stolen equipment they were able to partially dismantle the track. Their original thought had been that the driver would see the dismantled track and stop the train. But trains don't stop that easily.

The impact of this emergency stop split the engine and the impact caused the carriages to fall onto their sides. The engineer was killed as was the fireman as the engine overturned and crushed them.

Public Domain Image

But although the gang were surprised at the horror of this attack they continued and stole $3,000 (about $65,000 now) from the safe and $1,000 in jewellery from the passengers. They explained to the passengers that they had not planned on hurting any of them.

But later train robberies were focused on the safes in the baggage cars and not stealing anything from the passengers on the trains. This helped with Edward's newspaper image of Jesse as a 'Robin Hood' figure although we do not know if he did actually share his 'booty' with anyone other than the gang members.

In 1874, not only had Jesse married his sweetheart Zee, but the gang had now come to the attention of the Pinkerton Detective Agency. This Chicago based agency worked mainly against 'urban professional criminals'. This business opportunity had arisen due to the need for criminals to be caught and brought to justice.

Allan Pinkerton, the founder of the Pinkerton Detective agency, opened branches all over the West and his business of chasing and capturing outlaws really began. Thanks to the James–Younger Gang, Butch Cassidy, and many others, the Pinkertons were kept busy.

The James–Younger Gang's tactics had the support of many former Confederate soldiers and had so far managed to elude the Pinkertons sent to arrest them. Pinkerton's agents often worked undercover as Confederate soldiers and sympathizers to gather military intelligence.

Public Domain Image
Zerelda (Zee)

Pinkerton was hired by the railroad express companies to track down the outlaw Jesse James, but after Pinkerton failed to capture him, the railroad withdrew their financial support and Pinkerton continued to track Jesse at his own expense.

One agent was sent to Zerelda Samuel's farm was soon found dead, with two other agents dying in a gunfight with the Youngers.

Public Domain Image
Allan Pinkerton

This was not the news that the founder of the Pinkertons, Allan Pinkerton wanted to hear and decided to take on the mantle himself. Now it was personal. After a 'tip-off' Pinkerton targeted the James farm with the help of former Unionists.

They had heard that the James boys were there and on 25th January, 1875 Pinkerton headed out there too. Hiding outside they could see movement within the kitchen of the farm and the agents threw in lighted turpentine balls through the windows, plus an incendiary device, in the shape of a 33lb bomb, into the house. It had devastating effects.

Jesse's younger brother, Archie, was killed and Zerelda lost one of her arms. Pinkerton denied that his intentions had been to cause damage this way. But it was later discovered that this had been his intentions all along, when a letter was found to confirm this.

But the robberies continued despite having a new opponent in the Pinkertons. One particular robbery at the First National Bank of Northfield, Minnesota, in September 1876 caused the death of two gang members when it all went horribly wrong.

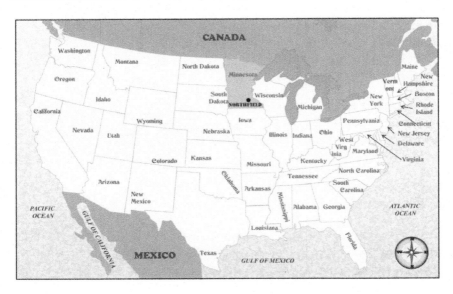

In order to rob the bank, the gang had split into two groups, one to enter the bank and the other to watch and wait from the outside. Bob Younger, Frank James and Charlie Pitts entered the bank, and Jesse James, Cole and Jim Younger, Bill Stiles and Clell Miller waited outside.

But inside the bank they were met with resistance as the acting cashier, Joseph Lee Heywood, refused to open the safe saying that it had a time lock and could not be opened. This was untrue and a very brave statement to make to the gang. He was threatened and beaten but he bravely continued his refusal to open the safe. A bank teller, Alonzo Bunker, saw a chance of escape and took it but was wounded in the shoulder as he left.

J. L. HEYWOOD,
The "HERO" of NORTHFIELD BANK,
KILLED SEPT 7TH 1876,

Public Domain Image

Once local citizens realised a robbery was in progress, a battle started between the townspeople of Northfield and the remaining gang members. Two were killed outright, Clell Miller and Bill Chadwell (alias Bill Stiles). The three Younger brothers managed to get away but were injured. The James brothers escaped to but were also injured.

What the gang didn't realise was the safe was already opened and that bloodshed was totally unnecessary. Heywood, as brave as he was, was shot in the head by a gang member as the gang escaped from the bank.

Two weeks after the Northfield robbery the Younger brothers were again wounded and Charlie Pitts was killed in a gunfight with the posse that had chased them since the robbery. The Younger brothers surrendered and pleaded guilty to murder. A grand jury charged them with first degree murder, robbery and assault with deadly weapons. They pleaded guilty and were sentenced to life in Minnesota Territorial Prison. Bob Younger died in prison while Cole and Jim gained parole in 1901 after serving 25 years.

Frank and Jesse escaped and the James-Younger gang was no more.

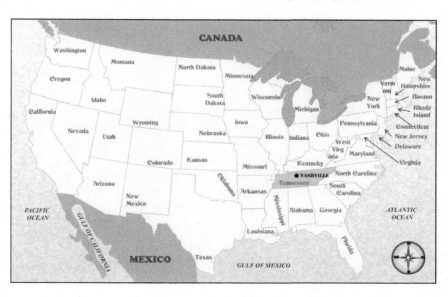

Having escaped, Frank and Jesse lived rather peacefully on a farm in Nashville, Tennessee. But this wasn't the life for Jesse and he soon started to get restless.

He recruited new members for his new gang consisting of Tucker Basham, Bill Ryan, Wood and Clarence Hite and Dick Liddil. But this was not successful. The gang members were not guerrilla tactics trained and were soon caught. Frank and Jesse tried a name change and Jesse became Thomas Howard and Frank adopted the name B. J. Woodson.

Public Domain Image
Frank and Jesse James

In 1879/1880 they carried out various train, store and stagecoach robberies. But Bill Ryan wasn't all that good at being discrete and bragged about their exploits getting himself arrested and Tucker Basham was captured by a posse. This instigated Frank and Jesse heading for the hills just in-case.

Train robberies were attempted again in September 1881 but the Chicago and Alton Railroad became Jesse's last train robbery as the safe was all but empty.

Due to the increase in train robberies and hearing that Frank and Jesse were back in business again, the Governor of Missouri, T. T. Crittenden offered a reward of $10,000 and gave Clay County sheriff, James Timberlake, the job of finding them.

He successfully arrested Clarence Hite, whilst Wood Hite had been killed in a shoot-out over a woman by gang member Dick Liddil.

Public Domain Image

T. T. Crittenden

Charley and Bob Ford, were also members of Jesse's new gang but Bob was not exactly accepted as a gang member. He was contacted by Timberlake who offered him a reward if he delivered Jesse.

Public Domain Image

James Timberlake

This was a great idea and both Charley and Bob agreed to help.

Jesse by now was living with his family in St. Joseph, Missouri. Bob and Charley were living there too and seemed like part of the family.

But Jesse had started to become increasingly suspicious of the motives of the Ford brothers, and even the brothers themselves felt that he knew he was going to be betrayed.

Public Domain Image

But instead of bringing the subject to the table, one particular morning on 3rd April, 1882, Jesse is said to have removed his guns and laid them down, got a chair, stood on it to dust a picture over the fireplace. With his back to them, Bob Ford used this opportunity and shot Jesse three times in the back of the head.

Public Domain Image

Charles Ford

Public Domain Image

Robert Ford

The Ford brothers surrendered themselves to the authorities. Eventually. They were charged with first degree murder, pleaded guilty, sentenced to death by hanging, and then pardoned in a very short space of time.

Bob used his fame to pose for photographs as the 'man who killed Jesse James'.

Public Domain Image

Edward O'Kelley

Bob Ford was killed in 1892 in a saloon dispute by Edward O'Kelley. O'Kelley became known as "the man who killed the man who killed Jesse James". No one knows why he wanted to kill Ford.

On 4th October, 1882 Frank James walked into Crittenden's office and surrendered. He was tried and acquitted despite having been involved in many killings.

Bob Younger died in prison on 15th September, 1889 aged 36 years. Cole and Jim Younger were paroled in 1901 but Jim committed suicide in 1902 aged 54 years. Cole was pardoned in 1903 under the proviso that he 'never returned to Minnesota' and instead he joined a Wild West show. He died in 1916 aged 72 years.

144

Public Domain Image

Frank never returned to crime and died in 1915 aged 72 years, at the family home.

Public Domain Image

Jesse was 34 years old when he was killed.

WILD BILL HICKOK

James Butler Hickok, of the Wild Bill Hickok fame, made his mark not only as a gunfighter, soldier, scout, lawman, gambler, actor and showman, but was involved in many a shoot-out during his life.

He has been immortalised by the stories about him, allegedly stories he potentially exaggerated for effect. He had always been a good shot from an early age but in 1855 aged 18 years, after a fight with another boy resulted in both boys falling into a canal.

Public Domain Image

He, like his opponent, thought the other was dead. This led him to flee to the Kansas Territory where he joined an antislavery group called the 'Jaywalkers'. It was with this group that he met a very young William Cody (Buffalo Bill to be).

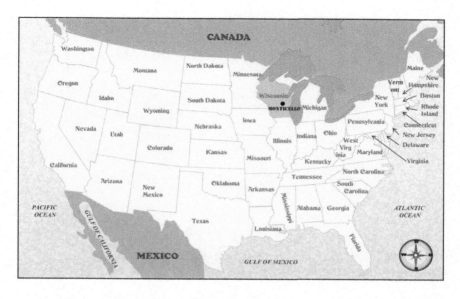

In 1858, at the age of 21 years, he was elected as one of four constables of Monticello Township. Another part of his life was taken up by becoming part of an off shoot of the Pony Express, the Russell, Majors and Waddell Freight Company. It was during this time that he encountered a bear while driving a freight team. Apparently the bear and its cubs had blocked the road. Hickok approached the bear and shot it in the head but the bullet glanced off the bear's skull annoying her rather a lot. The bear attacked Hickok and crushed him under her body. Hickok fired again but only managed from his awkward prone position to shoot the bear in the paw. Things did not improve after that shot either.

The bear took a nice big bite out of Hickok's arm which gave him, painfully, the leeway needed to get his knife and slash at the bear's throat killing it. But Hickok was in a bad way and naturally it took quite some time to regain his strength again working as a stable hand for the freight company at Rock Creek Station while he recovered.

Public Domain Image

147

He soon got his strength back and various shoot outs occurred, but one in particular he did apologise to the widow about killing her husband and offered her compensation of $35 as this was all the money he had.

In 1863 Hickok met up with Buffalo Bill Cody again when he worked for the provost Marshall of southwest Missouri as part of the Springfield Detective Agency. The role required him to *seek out soldiers who drank while on duty, make sure that hotels kept to the requirements of the liquor licenses, and finding anyone who owed money to the Union Army.*

Public Domain Image

Public Domain Image

Davis Tutt

One famous Hickok shootout got Hickok arrested for murder. Gambling was a serious business and debts from gambling were sometimes paid in kind. This time Hickok had lost a watch that he particularly liked and asked his opponent Davis Tutt, not to wear it in public. Tutt agreed and apparently soon changed his mind. There was only one solution. A shootout.

Public Domain Image

Facing each other in Springfield's town square, they both shot. Tutt missed but Hickok didn't. He was arrested for murder, but later reduced to manslaughter with a $2,000 bail. The trial happened on 3rd August, 1865 and the Judge Sempronius H. Boyd advised the jury that they *"could not find Hickok acted in self defence if he could have reasonable avoided the fight."* But he continued by saying, *"if they felt the threat of danger was real and imminent, then they could apply the unwritten law of 'fair fight' and acquit."* They cleared Hickok of all charges but the public were unhappy about it all.

It was soon after this incident that a journalist named Colonel George Ward Nichols, probably the creator of the legend that was Hickok, wrote of the daring does of Wild Bill Hickok and the 'hundreds' of men whom Hickok had killed. And a legend was born.

Public Domain Image

Wild Bill Hickok

Public Domain Image

By 1865 Hickok failed to gain election as sheriff in Springfield and left for the role of deputy federal marshal of Fort Riley, Kansas, serving also as a scout for General George A. Custer and his 7th Cavalry.

Also in 1865 Hickok tried his hand at showmanship with the outdoor demonstration of *'The Daring Buffalo Chasers of the Plains'*. As the show was outdoors it was easy for the spectators to watch without paying and ended up as a failure for Hickok and his team.

By December 1867, Hickok was deputy US Marshall in Hays City, Kansas, working with Buffalo Bill Cody to bring in Union army deserters which they did.

His scouting role continued for the 10th Cavalry, with a return to Hays County and election as City Marshall of Hays and Sheriff of Ellis County, Kansas. But this role didn't make him a popular bloke as many sought to kill him.

One man, called Bill Mulvey, drunk and disorderly in town was told to behave. He didn't. He was out to shoot the sheriff. Hickok tricked him into thinking there were others behind him ready to shoot him, and when Mulvey turned to look, Hickok shot him in the head. Problem solved.

JOHN WESLEY HARDIN MEETS WILD BILL

One particular gunfighter appeared on the scene around this time; John Wesley Hardin. He had at least 27 killings under his belt. He was not a man to be tangled with. Hickok was Marshall in Abilene now and the year is now 1871.

Public Domain Image

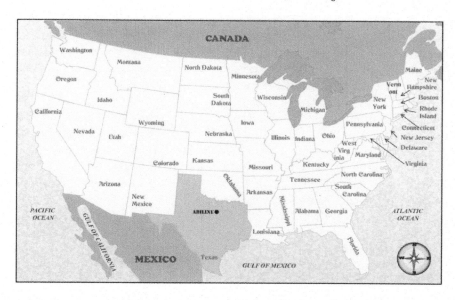

Hardin claims to have been a friend of Hickok's in Abilene, whilst Hickok claimed that he did not know that the man named Wesley Clemmons (Hardin's alias) was John Wesley Hardin. Hickok simply asked Hardin to hand over his guns and stay out of trouble in Abilene. Hardin agreed.

But Hardin's killings caught up with him quickly when he killed a man called Charles Cougar because 'he snored too loud'. Hardin left before Hickok could arrest him.

Hardin was known as a ruthless gunman of his day. He had a long held grudge against anti-slavery and a very quick temper. He started early at the age of 14 by stabbing a fellow student who taunted him, also killing a slave and an 'Indian' for practise.

History says that he killed 42 men. He was arrested for one of these murders in January, 1871 and escorted to trial by Texas lawmen Edward Stakes and Jim Smalley to Waco for trial. Stakes left to get food, Smalley started to taunt Hardin. Hardin pretended to be upset. Unbeknown to Smalley, Hardin had a hidden pistol and after untying himself, he shot and killed Smalley.

Hardin escaped the law, changed his name and lived in Florida until his capture on a train heading back to Pensacola from Alabama. The Texas Rangers had become involved in the hunt for him and he was spotted boarding a train in Pensacola.

On the train Texas Ranger John Armstrong walked into the carriage that Hardin was in, spotted him but Hardin could not get his gun out quick enough. It was stuck in the holster belt. Armstrong clubbed him until he was out for the count. A wanted man was now caught.

Hardin was tried in 1878 and sentenced to 25 years in Huntsville prison and served 17 years. He tried to escape many times but eventually settled down to prison life, and studied law writing an autobiography about the era. He was released 1894, returned to Gonzales, Texas, and found life outside hard. On 16th March, 1894 Hardin was pardoned passed the Texas state's bar examination and gained his license to practise law.

Although alone now that his wife had died, he headed to El Paso Texas but was still a marked man.

Peace officer John Selman and his son John Selman Jnr. arrested Hardin's current girlfriend and because of this Hardin threatened to kill them both. But they got there first and while Hardin was shooting dice in the saloon, Selman Snr. shot him in the back of the head. Then to make sure he shot him twice more just in-case.

Selman Snr. was arrested for murder and stood trial. Claiming it was self-defence, a hung jury meant he was 'released on bond pending re-trial'. He too was killed before the retrial.

But Hardin's life ended on 19th August, 1895 in El Paso at the age of 42 years.

But Hickok's life as gunfighter also came to a very abrupt and sad end too, in 1871 when he accidentally shot his Special Deputy Marshall Mike Williams. Williams had run to Hickok's aid as a shootout between a saloon owner, Phil Coe and Hickok himself had occurred.

Coe really had it in for Hickok and was determined to 'finish him off'. But Hickok tried to arrest him for firing off his gun in the town and was forced to shoot and kill Coe when he turned his gun on Hickok.

John Wesley Hardin, killed in El Paso, Texas, August 19, 1895.

Public Domain Image

Public Domain Image

Seeing someone else running towards him Hickok fired again. Only this time he had shot one of his constables, Deputy Williams, who appeared in the wrong spot at the wrong time and got the full force from the pistol killing him. Williams had been running to help Hickok. Hickok was relieved of his duties as Marshall at Abilene, Kansas and the devastating effect of the shootings stayed with him.

By 1873, Buffalo Bill Cody and Texas Jack Omohundro offered Hickok a role in the Wild West Shows. He tried but it didn't work. He did not like 'acting' and literally hated the limelight or any kind of light shining on him on stage.

Public Domain Image
Buffalo Bill Cody

Public Domain Image
Texas Jack Omohundro

It was now 1876 and Hickok was a sick man. He was diagnosed as having glaucoma which had serious impact on his ability to shoot anymore. He had become a compulsive gambler and a marked man. He had made himself into a legend. The dime novels had glorified his past and he helped by expanding on his exploits. There were many out to get him. And he spent the remainder of his life constantly looking out for himself. He was only 39 years old but his decline was a steep one with various arrests for vagrancy.

He tried to settle down in marital bliss in March 1876, but married life was not for him and he left his new bride, Agnes Thatcher Lake, after a few months and went to seek his fortune in gold in South Dakota.

There were many out to get him. And he spent the remainder of his life constantly looking backwards for that faster gun. Always sitting with his back to the wall in the saloon while gambling, to protect himself, but still telling his tall tales to keep his legendary reputation going to anyone who would listen. It was still 1876 and Hickok was in Deadwood by now.

Deadwood had appeared as many 'boomtowns' of that era did. This time because of the gold found on the Sioux sacred land of the Black Hills.

Thousands upon thousands of gold seekers and miners arrived and set up a mining camp calling it Deadwood. And the name stuck.

Gold that Custer had originally found during an expedition after the Fort Laramie Treaty of 1868 was reneged once the gold was found.

Wyatt Earp was there for a spell making himself a fortune in 1877. The Sundance Kid spent time in jail there before he became famous, and Calamity Jane is reputed to have been busy as a prostitute there too.

Everything they could possibly want as far as supplies and anything else for that matter was concerned, at an exorbitant fee of course, could be bought there. With many other ways to lose your hard earned money, with the gamblers and cardsharps that frequented these places.

Deadwood was, and still is, one of those towns. Only now it's all for show to entertain the tourists. But in its heyday it was buzzing.

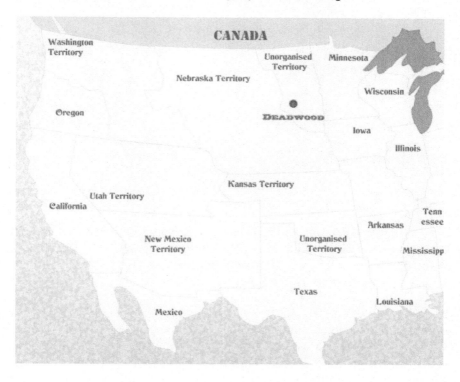

Public Domain Image   Public Domain Image

CyArk
https://commons.wikimedia.org/wiki/File:Cyark_Deadwood_Hickock.jpg
Cyark Deadwood Hickock
https://creativecommons.org/licenses/by-sa/3.0/legalcode

Public Domain Image
Jack McCall

On 1st August, 1876, Jack McCall was in the Nuttal and Mann's saloon in Deadwood and found a table and Hickok to play poker. And McCall lost everything. Hickok offered him money for breakfast and advised him not to play again until he could afford to.

Next day, 2nd August, 1876, still smarting from his loss McCall, still drunk, went back to the bar and found Hickok playing poker again. Hickok was sitting with his back to the door which was most unusual for him. He was unprotected. McCall saw this as an opportunity for revenge and drew his .45 calibre revolver and shouted "Damn you take that", and shot Hickok twice in the back of the head. Hickok was 39 years old.

When McCall was asked later why he didn't face up to Hickok he said "I didn't want to commit suicide". It took two trials but McCall was hanged on 1st March, 1877.

Hickok's last poker hand consisted of two black aces and two black eights which later came to be called the dead man's hand.

His legend remains as many stars have immortalised him on film such as Gary Cooper, Charles Bronson, Jeff Bridges and Luke Hemsworth.

TOMBSTONE AND THE EARPS

Tombstone was originally nicknamed 'The Town Too Rough To Die' and was a huge boomtown with about 14,000 residents in the 1880s. Those residents, apparently, generated about $85 million in silver during the 1880s and with 110 saloons, 14 gambling halls, an ice cream parlour, bowling alley, opera house and numerous brothels. There was a lot of places that money changed hands.

Public Domain Image

Ed Schiefflin

History states that it started off with very humble beginnings as the founder of Tombstone, Ed Schiefflin, had been collecting rocks in the area which was Apache territory. Collecting rocks that he hoped held silver.

Looking for a bit of respite from the outdoors life, he sought shelter at Fort Huachuca and they were curious as to why he was living on such dangerous Apache land. He answered simply, he was collecting rocks. It is said that the response was, "You keep fooling around out there amongst them Apache and the only rock you'll find will be your tombstone." Hence the name. And silver was found.

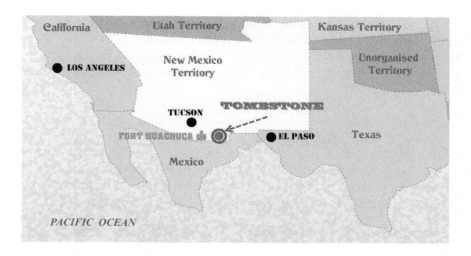

Public Domain Image

Wyatt Earp

The Earps arrived at end of 1879. Wyatt Berry Stapp Earp, James Cooksey Earp, Virgil Walter Earp and Morgan Seth Earp.

Tombstone wasn't quite established then but by the next year its population had multiplied making Tombstone a huge mining town. And the home of the biggest, most well-known gun fight at the OK Corral.

Prior to this Wyatt had a fairly chequered past with his involvement in many varying careers.

Public Domain Image

Wyatt Earp

At age 13 years he ran away from his home in Illinois, trying to join the Union Army alongside his brothers Newton, James and Virgil. But each time he tried this, his father Nicholas brought him back to the farm where they lived to tend to his duties alongside his other brothers Morgan and Warren.

After the American Civil War, Newton, James and Virgil returned to the family home now in California. Although still too young to work, Wyatt assisted his brother, Virgil, on the Phineas Banning stage coach line in California when he was 16 years old. In 1866, this role increased when he became a teamster transporting cargo from Wilmington through Las Vegas, Nevada into Salt Lake City in Utah. A total of about 720 miles.

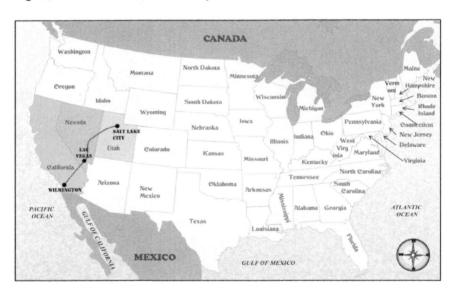

He also became part of the Union Pacific Railroad expansion in 1868 and transported much needed supplies to keep the railroad going. This role, and the people he dealt with, gave him a new education in gambling and boxing and he became known for officiating at boxing matches refereeing a fight between John Shanssey and Prof. Mike Donovan in front of a huge crowd of spectators.

Lamar, Missouri, soon became the home base for the Wyatt family in 1869 and it's here that Wyatt's father, Nicholas, resigned from his role as constable of the township there.

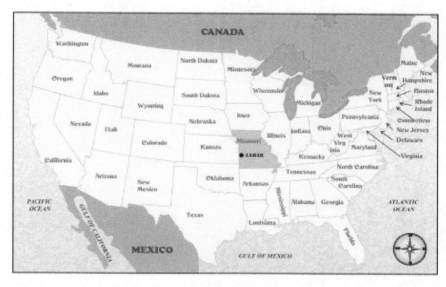

Wyatt was appointed constable in his place in November 1869. And it was also here that Wyatt met and married Urilla Sutherland. But despite being in marital bliss and building his own house for his new wife and family, Urilla died suddenly in 1870. Some say she died just before she was due to have their first child, others that she had typhoid fever. But after that things started to go downhill for Wyatt.

Public Domain Image
Urilla Sutherland

Wyatt faced many financial and legal problems and was even charged with horse stealing at one stage in 1871, but escaped before he was arrested. It was at this stage of his life it is said that he met up with Wild Bill Hickok whom he regarded with respect, and a man called Bat Masterson.

But it got worse in 1872 as he, Morgan and a man called George Randall, were arrested for 'keeping and being found in a house of ill-fame'.

Public Domain Image

Both Earps were arrested for the same crime a couple of times after this and Wyatt was even linked to a brothel that his brother James ran in Wichita. Wyatt's common law wife, Sally Heckell, and James's wife ran the brothel and historians think that Wyatt may have been a 'bouncer' there.

Wyatt's life seemed to revolve around spending much time in saloons, gambling houses, and brothels, with arrests on several occasions for consorting with prostitutes.

But this life was not what Wyatt was looking for. He needed more and eventually got an opportunity for change when he helped a Wichita police officer catch a thief who had stolen a wagon and horse.

This capture brought Wyatt to the attention of the Wichita police and he was asked to join the Wichita's marshal's office in 1875 as a policeman. And with Wichita being a railroad terminal for cattle drives, the town became very rowdy when the cowhands arrived. Lawmen were needed. But even this came to a sudden end when Wyatt, even though he was an excellent lawman, was accused of using his status as lawman to hire his brothers as lawmen too. Wyatt wasn't re-elected. Off he went on his travels again.

This time in Dodge City, Kansas in 1876, Wyatt became the deputy town Marshall, arriving with his girlfriend Mattie Blaylock, a prostitute. Even this role didn't hold him for long as in 1876-1877, Wyatt and Morgan travelled together hoping to strike gold in the area around Deadwood, Dakota. But by the time they had arrived, all the prime land had already gone in mining claims so Wyatt came up with a money making plan. He bought every last scrap of wood and hauled it into camp at Deadwood and sold it for a fortune, as the winter was a hard one and wood was just like gold to the residents there. Not only for heat, building shelter but also as props needed in gold mining.

By 1877 Wyatt had returned to Dodge City.

Dodge City was another railhead for cattle drives and Wyatt's reputation gained him further promotion as the City Marshall in Dodge City in 1877.

You've seen in all the cowboy films when the gunslinger walks, confidently and sometimes threateningly, around town with his guns held in his holster belted around his hips and his hand not too far away from his guns ready to draw quickly. Well apparently it wasn't like that at all.

At first it was, particularly in Dodge City, that living there seemed to encourage trouble arriving in the shape of gunslingers, buffalo hunters, railroad workers and soldiers. Gun fights were common and the people of Dodge City were scared, naturally.

Many of the peace officers had been run out of town or left for their own safety, so Wyatt arriving with Bat Masterson and a couple of others must have seemed like a God-send to the residents. A new 'gun-toting rule' was quickly established and if you were in the wrong part of Dodge wearing or using a gun you were jailed. And it quickly helped solve the problems in Dodge.

And the rule spread. Carrying guns within the town was banned in places from Dodge City to Tombstone. Concealed or otherwise. The movies might be historically wrong but they look good, and it's the way everyone perceives it to be. And from what I have discovered, people entering these places seemed quite happy to hand over their guns when they arrived, collecting them later when they left. But despite being fairly peaceable in town, not everyone followed the rules or there would have been no need for men like Wyatt.

But Wyatt seemed to continually move between Deadwood, Dodge City and Tombstone quite regularly and while he was back at Dodge City, Wyatt was given a temporary commission and tasked with hunting down 'Dirty' Dave Rudabaugh (23 years old) who is said to have robbed the Santa Fe Railroad Construction site. If you remember Rudabaugh was a member of Billy the Kid's gang.

Public Domain Image
Dirty Dave

'Dirty' Dave gained his novel nickname due to the fact that he washed rarely and wore the same clothes every day.

Now Wyatt was on the hunt for Rudabaugh. And hunt he did. And in the long process of hunting him down, he arrived at Fort Griffin and was told that a man called Doc Holliday, a gambler, may know of his whereabouts.

It was here that Wyatt met this well-known gambler called Doc Holliday. Doc Holliday had apparently played cards with Rudabaugh who had since left. Doc Holliday wasn't sure but he thought that Rudabaugh and his gang were heading back to Kansas.

Armed with this new information Wyatt telegraphed the Sheriff at Ford County to warn him that the gang could be heading their way, and apparently a posse was formed just in-case. Sheriff Bat Masterson was in charge and eventually caught up with the gang and they were arrested. Rudabaugh informed on his gang members and was released and headed to New Mexico.

Public Domain Image
Doc Holliday

Wyatt and Mattie returned to Dodge City and not long after this Doc Holliday arrived with his common law wife, Big Nose Kate. Dodge City was still the place to let off steam after a cattle drive and with Doc Holliday's help, Wyatt was able to stem the trouble there before it got really bad.

Public Domain Image
**Mary Katherine Horony
(Big Nose Kate)**

A friendship developed between the two men and historians say that it all came from Doc Holliday saving Wyatt's life.

Ed Morrison and his friends needed some 'counselling' from Wyatt. This led to the saloon where Doc Holliday was playing cards. Morrison and his 'friends' had the 'draw' on Wyatt when he entered the saloon, but Doc Holliday simply drew his gun, which he had hidden under the table, put it to Morrison's head and advised him to lower his gun telling him to advise his 'friends' to do the same. Morrison did as he was asked and Wyatt was eternally grateful. Morrison and his men were locked up, and this was the start of the friendship between the Wyatt and Doc Holliday.

Public Domain Image
Virgil Earp

Public Domain Image
**Bat Masterson standing
Wyatt Earp seated**

Public Domain Image
Mattie Blaylock

This was also the time that Wyatt met up with policeman Bat Masterson.

165

By 1879 Dodge City was becoming a much calmer place to live and I think this made Wyatt unsettled yet again. Virgil, the town constable in Prescott, Arizona, came to the rescue when he told Wyatt about the silver mining opportunities in Tombstone. This was the news Wyatt needed and soon after Wyatt, Virgil, James and their wives arrived in Tombstone. They, like many others, were hoping to make their fortune.

Doc Holliday stayed in Prescott nearby as he was happy with the gambling opportunities there.

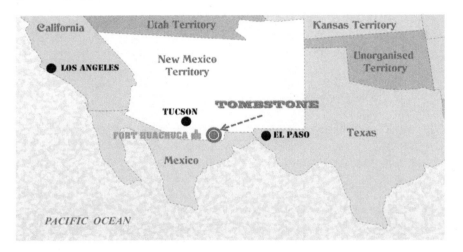

The three Earp's tried their hand at mining claims and buying small properties trying to establish themselves as business men but without success. Instead Wyatt worked on the Wells Fargo stagecoaches riding shotgun when they were transporting strong boxes.

In 1880 Virgil, the Deputy US Marshall, was asked to track down the 'Cowboys' who were accused of stealing army mules.

The outlaw Clanton Gang had been terrorising the area for some time and getting away with it too. When the Earps arrived they were none too happy.

The gang, or the 'Cowboys' was made up of "Old Man" Clanton his sons, Ike, Billy and Phin, Tom and Frank McLaury, Curly Bill Brocius, Johnny Ringo, Pete Spence and several others.

| Ike Clanton | Frank McLaury | Billy Claiborne | Tom McLaury |

They had been involved in cattle rustling in Old Mexico for quite some time, moving their plunder to their ranch on the San Pedro River. They managed to keep this enterprise going because of the help they got from the Cochise County Sheriff, John Behan, who they paid regularly. Now mules were going missing. Until the Earps came.

In order to try and stem this, Virgil requested that he had help from his brothers Wyatt and Morgan. This was agreed and both were deputised. They found the mules but the whole incident started the feud between the 'Cowboys' and the Earps from then on.

In 1879 Wyatt had met 18 year old Josephine "Josie" Sarah Marcus while in Tombstone. She was working with a travelling theatre group and was Sheriff John Behan's girlfriend. Wyatt and Josie hit it off, much to Sheriff Behan's displeasure. Not only were the Earps targeting the 'Cowboys' and stopping his extra funds, but Wyatt was after his girlfriend too. Wyatt's girlfriend of the time, Mattie, was very dependent on laudanum which was now placing a strain on their relationship. With this extra competition for Josie's affections, Sheriff Behan was now taking this very personally.

In February 1881 Wyatt ran for sheriff but was defeated by John Behan. Wyatt was without a potential job now, so Wyatt moved onto the gambling tables instead and encouraged people like Bat Masterson to help him work the tables there which he did for a while. Plus the Earp brothers' mining claims had started to show a bit of a profit too.

Life continued and they got used to the fact that many disliked them, particularly the Clantons. Wyatt joined a posse to find the 'Cowboys' who had robbed a stagecoach. Wyatt's hope was that if successful, this could lead to him being elected as sheriff.

The 'Cowboys' continued their various robberies, and the Earps continued pursuing them to bring them to justice. Seeking support from Ike Clanton, who he felt was part of the 'Cowboys', Wyatt offered him reward money if he cooperated. Ike agreed but soon became rather anxious that if his association with Wyatt was found out by the other 'Cowboys' then he wouldn't be around for very long.

This just made the situation a lot worse and Ike Clanton was quite happy to broadcast around Tombstone how he felt about the Earps once he had had a drink or two inside him. His bravado sent out the message that they wanted to see the Earps settled in Boot Hill very soon, and they were not afraid to use their guns whenever they were in town.

In 1881 the Earps and the Clantons were most definitely enemies. Virgil took over as acting Marshall when the original Marshall left town in a hurry and Virgil enforced the law quite strongly. Arrests were made which instigated threats of further violence specifically towards the Earp brothers. And these threats came from the McLaurys.

The bad blood between the 'Cowboys' and the Earps just seemed to increase daily. Threatening to kill the Earps continuously over the weeks that led up to the Gunfight at OK Corral, just kept the hatred built up for the Clantons and the other 'Cowboys'. As far as the 'Cowboys' were concerned there was no one to stop them. Or try to stop them.

In Tombstone Virgil, the town sheriff, asked for help from Wyatt and Morgan (Morgan was classed as a special policeman) and Doc Holliday, as the tension in Tombstone had increased. Virgil knew that this was not going to blow over without a fight; a now famous gunfight.

Public Domain Image

About 3.00pm on 26th October, 1881, the Earps and Doc Holliday headed to Fremont Street which is where the gunfight actually happened and this was next to the OK Corral. It took 30 shots and approximately 30 seconds for the Earps to win the gunfight. It is unknown who shot first.

During the shooting Tom and Frank McClaury and Billy Clanton were killed. Billy Claiborne ran away. **'Morgan was wounded by a shot across his back that nicked both shoulder blades and a vertebra. Virgil was shot through the calf, and Holliday was grazed by a bullet'.** Wikipedia The only one not hurt was Wyatt.

On 29th October, Ike Clanton filed charges for murder against the Earps and Doc Holliday. They were arrested and held in jail. After a 30 day hearing the Earps and Doc Holliday were acquitted.

Witnesses said that the 'Cowboys' didn't have guns with them. Odd that the Wyatt brothers were shot. But it didn't stop there. The rest of the 'Cowboys' were planning revenge.

Public Domain Image

Billy Clanton on the right/McLaury brothers beside him. This was taken by C. S. Fly

Surprisingly enough, during my research for this book I have discovered that an Old West photographer Camillus 'Buck' Sydney Fly (C. S. Fly) was an eyewitness to the Gunfight at the OK Corral which actually took place just outside his photographic studio.

Public Domain Image

His fame as a photographer also included pictures of the life of miners during the silver mining boom in Tombstone and not to forget the remarkable pictures of Geronimo's surrender in 1886.

Public Domain Image   Public Domain Image   Public Domain Image

He is said to have taken his camera with him on many occasions and the results were published in 'periodicals' of the day.

Sadly his work was destroyed by two fires burning his studio to the ground, but his images remaining are still a wonderful look at history as it was then.

Public Domain Image

Back in Tombstone life just seemed to be getting worse after the OK Corral and this led to the ambush of Virgil in 1881 which seriously injured him. Wyatt took on the role of deputy US Marshall as Virgil's injuries were too severe for him to continue working. And worse still the following year, in March, Morgan was ambushed and killed by his attackers.

These tragic repercussions led to, what is now known as the Earp Vendetta Ride. Wyatt was now the Deputy United States Marshal and deputised Holliday, Warren Earp, Sherman McMaster and 'Turkey Creek' Jack Johnson to join his posse for the Vendetta Ride.

Quite a few suspected that the 'Cowboys' were involved. Some were found, charged but later released, after intense searches by the Wyatt posse. Hoping as Wyatt did, that the law would win out and the 'Cowboys' would be brought to justice, never happened, and Wyatt decided that it was best to take charge of this himself.

Wyatt and the posse escorted the severely injured Virgil onto a train to take him back to his home to recoup. Also on board was the body of Morgan ready for his burial back home in Colton.

The posse spotted Ike Clanton and Frank Stilwell hanging around the station. Perhaps to try and 'finish off' Virgil. Who knows? The posse gave chase and Stilwell was killed while the other got away.

Sheriff Behan, on their return to Tombstone, tried to stop Wyatt's posse from continuing their quest of pursuit of the 'Cowboys'. This failed and Behan formed his own posse to pursue Wyatt instead.

Wyatt and his posse heard that another 'Cowboy', Florentino "Indian Charlie" Cruz, was at a woodcutting camp off the Chiricahua Road, below the South Pass of the Dragoon Mountains. And that's exactly where Wyatt and the posse headed for.

Many shots were fired and next morning Cruz was found dead.

Public Domain Image

June 10th, 1883: (L to R) Standing: William H. Harris, Luke Short, Bat Masterson, William F. Petillon
Seated: Charlie Bassett, Wyatt Earp, Michael Francis "Frank" McLean, and Cornelius "Neil" Brown

Chased but not caught by Cochise County Sheriff John Behan and his posse now on the Wyatt Earp trail, Wyatt headed east into New Mexico then onto Colorado in 1882.

In 1882 Wyatt joined Virgil in San Francisco and it is here that he met up again with Josie Marcus. Mattie had already died of an overdose of laudanum after she left Tombstone. But meeting up with Josie again seemed to be destiny for Wyatt as they appeared to be definitely right for each other and during their relationship, they found many money making opportunities wherever they could and were together for the next 47 years, reportedly never leaving each other's side. Wyatt continued his role as lawman occasionally but never stayed in one place for very long.

Virgil and his wife, Allie, moved to California where he became the town sheriff despite not having full use of his injured arm after the attack in

1881. Virgil died in October 1905 after a serious bout of pneumonia which he never really recovered from.

Ike Clanton was killed during an attempted robbery in June 1887. The last of the 'Cowboys' from the OK Corral.

Wyatt's moneymaking ventures however, included an alleged heavyweight boxing match that he apparently refereed and fixed on 2nd December, 1896, between Tom 'Sailor' Sharkey and Robert 'Ruby' Fitzsimmons. The fight was billed as the heavy weight championship of the world and Fitzsimmons was set as the best bet. This wasn't the first time Wyatt had refereed a boxing match but it appears to be the one remembered.

During the match, Fitzsimmons had the upper hand until it looked like Sharkey had been hit below the belt and the Wyatt stopped the fight. Wyatt awarded the fight to Sharkey and all hell broke loose.

Wyatt was accused of 'fixing' the fight and apparently betting on Sharkey himself. It was later revealed that boxing promoters did try to fix fights. This news and the fact that everyone accused Wyatt of betting on Sharkey did not help his reputation. A reputation that was tarnished from then on in and never recovered.

Fitzsimmons tried to have Wyatt's decision overturned by taking the matter to court, and it was here that evidence came out regarding promoters fixing fights.

The circumstances surrounding the fight were so bad that on 17th December, 1896 Judge Sanderson ruled that prize fighting was now illegal in San Francisco and could not decide who had actually won the fight. So Sharkey kept the winnings.

Many years later a Doctor B. Brookes Lee was accused of making it look like Sharkey had been fouled by Fitzsimmons, and he confessed to having done just that and had been paid handsomely for it too.

Public Domain Image

After a short stint at the Klondike Gold Rush in Alaska in 1897, a spell in San Francisco, and a general store for the Alaska Commercial Company, he and Josie, in 1899, went to Nome where they owned a saloon then another in Nevada and had a few gold mining claims too.

By 1900 Wyatt's brother, Warren, had been shot and killed in a saloon fight in Arizona. Of the brothers, he was thought to have a '*hasty quick temper*' and it was thought that he would 'meet a violent death'. It appears that the brothers were not wrong.

But Wyatt's colourful life continued and many business ventures were tried, some successful, some not.

In 1901 Josie and Wyatt sold out their business in Nome and left for Los Angeles with a lot of cash to spend. After a short stay they moved to Toponah, Nevada, and opened another saloon there as the gold and silver boom led to many miners arriving with much to spend.

After the rush finished, Wyatt and Josie moved to Goldfield Nevada in 1905 where Virgil and his family were living. They staked mining claims near Death Valley discovering gold and copper with other mining claims near the Whipple Mountains, California, at the 'Happy Days' gold mine.

At the age of 62 years, Wyatt was hired by the Los Angeles Police Department to work 'outside the law' finding criminals hiding in Mexico. He apparently did this rather too well and it led to his final confrontation when a group of surveyors that he and his posse were guarding from the American Trona Company, classed as claim jumpers by many others, were confronted by armed men from another company.

Wyatt is said to have shot at the feet of the Federal Receiver Stafford W. Austin and said while brandishing his rifle, ***"Back off or I'll blow you apart, or my name is not Wyatt Earp"***. This led to his arrest, and that of his posse, by a US Marshall for contempt of court alongside 27 others, but the arrest did not help the situation at all as the dispute between the surveyors and companies continued afterwards.

While spending a lot of time in Los Angeles, 1915 saw Wyatt turning his hand as an acting consultant and spending time meeting stars like Tom Mix, a well-known cowboy actor in the black and white silent days. Plus John Wayne, who at the time was a prop man and an extra in movies. Wyatt is said to have frequently visited the set of action movies directed by John Ford and became quite well known there and accepted. Charlie Chaplin is also said to have been 'impressed' by the former Tombstone Marshall.

In 1920 Wyatt was given the honorary title of Deputy Sheriff of San Bernardino County, California. But it wasn't long after in 1928 that Wyatt's health was really starting to fail. He was the last surviving Earp brother as James had died in 1926.

Wyatt tried to have the story of his life published and worked with a man called John Flood who tried to write Wyatt's life as he recalled it. It was finished in 1926 but was rejected by many publishers.

But that all changed after his death on 13th January, 1929 at the age of 80 years. Movies changed and stories about gangsters and outlaws became something sought after by the viewing public. They needed heroes to lift their lives and they got it. Especially with the story of the Earp brothers.

At Wyatt's funeral Tom Mix was one of the pall bearers, and it is said that John Wayne also attended the funeral. And newspapers of the day said that Tom Mix cried. Josie didn't attend.

DOC HOLLIDAY

But you can't talk about the Earp brothers without mentioning Doc Holliday. He too is a famous name in the American West and closely associated with the Gunfight at OK Corral. Even though his beginnings were pointing him in a completely different direction.

John Henry ("Doc") Holliday was born 14th August, 1851, in a place called Griffin, in Georgia. His parents, Henry Burroughs Holliday and Alice Jane Holliday, were delighted with his arrival as it was only a year since they had lost their first baby, a daughter.

His birth, although celebrated, had a trauma attached as he was born with a cleft palate and needed surgery to correct this. It affected his speech and his mother spent some quite considerable time helping him to develop his confidence and how to try to overcome his speech problems. This led to a very close relationship between them, and her death from tuberculosis in 1866, devastated him. He had been a good student and this tragedy provided an increased focus for his knowledge of maths and science just to help him cope with her loss.

Public Domain Image

He soon became a student of the University of Pennsylvania Dental School, in Philadelphia, where he graduated in 1872. He worked as a dentist in the south for a spell but history has it that he left the south rather quickly for Dallas, Texas, and the only explanation historians have recorded is that he too was diagnosed with tuberculosis in 1873 and left for a climate with drier air to try and help his condition. He was 23 years old.

He did continue his life as a dentist but something else was starting to interest him. And it seemed and easier life than that of a dentist. He discovered gambling and drinking and he was good at both. This new career did come with some complications as he was indicted for illegal gambling, arrested for gunfire and assault to murder a saloon keeper but found not guilty and released. Although he did continue his dental practise in Dallas, his condition brought on extreme bouts of coughing and his dental practise started to decline because of this.

Soon, his gambling habits were his life and by the mid 1870s he had a reputation for playing cards and fighting. Fighting through shoot outs too and on many occasions was involved with wounding his opponent or being acquitted for 'troublemakers' in saloons.

Public Domain Image

After escaping the charge of murder in Dallas, (unconfirmed in history) Doc Holliday went on the move. One stop over brought him to Fort Griffin in 1877 and the John Shanssey saloon where he met Mary Katherine Horony (Big Nose Kate) who was a dance hall girl and occasionally a prostitute. She appears to have been the only woman in Doc Holliday's life.

Public Domain Image

Life took an important turn in 1877 when outlaws, led by 'Dirty' Dave Rudabaugh, robbed the Santa Fe railroad. On their trail was Deputy US Marshall Wyatt Earp. Speaking to the owner of the hotel Wyatt was advised to speak to Doc Holliday who may know where Rudabaugh had gone. Information given by Doc Holliday and duly passed on by Wyatt to Bat Masterson, Wyatt was now destined to go to Dodge City. As was Doc Holliday where he opened another dental practise. And Doc Holliday and Wyatt's life was soon to become intertwined.

Wyatt was now Assistant City Marshall in Dodge City and it was during his time that he was trying to keep the peace in Dodge City. It was a rowdy place and the cowboys were there to have fun. Shooting the place up was fun to them, and Wyatt followed them into the saloon bursting in quickly to surprise them, only he got the surprise as they all turned and trained their guns at him.

Public Domain Image

Doc Holliday

Ed Morrison, one of the cowboys that Wyatt had already had dealings with, had Wyatt in his sights. Until Doc Holliday, playing cards at a nearby table, drew his gun and put it to Morrison's head and advised him to lower his gun and tell the others to do the same. They complied, and Wyatt lived to tell the tale and very grateful he was too I would imagine. And this was the start of the friendship between the two men.

178

After a stint in Las Vegas where he was acquitted for killing a man in a saloon, Doc Holliday followed Wyatt to Tombstone, Arizona, a booming mining and frontier town near the Mexican border. Wyatt had told him of the marvellous opportunities in silver mining and he soon arrived there too.

Public Domain Image

As friendships go, it appears that Holliday's relationship with Big Nose Kate might have been less than 'made in heaven'. At one stage she got drunk, Holliday threw her out, and for revenge she signed an affidavit implicating Holliday in the attempted robbery and murder of passengers on the Kinnear and Company stage coach in March 1881. It was carrying $26,000 in silver bullion (about $697,000 now). The alcohol was given to her in vast quantities by County Sheriff Johnny Behan and Milt Joyce and it looked like a great opportunity for them to 'solve' a crime and for her to gain revenge. It worked and Holliday was now a marked man.

But thanks to the Earp's finding witnesses who could swear to Doc Holliday's whereabouts which was elsewhere at the time of the crime, the charges were dismissed. And once Big Nose Kate sobered up, she too confessed that she had been coerced into signing something she did not understand. Holliday was released.

On 19th April, 1881 Tombstone city council pass a ruling that anyone carrying a gun/rifle or bowie knife had to hand in their weapons to the local saloon or livery stable. And it was in Tombstone that Doc Holliday really became the legend that many people know of when he was part of the Gunfight at the OK Corral.

On 26th October, 1881, Doc Holliday and the Earps found themselves in a gunfight with Ike and Billy Clanton, and Frank and Tom McLaury.

Public Domain Image   Public Domain Image   Public Domain Image   Public Domain Image

Ike Clanton   **Frank McLaury**   **Billy Claiborne**   **Tom McLaury**

It is said to have only lasted for about 30-seconds but it is now the most legendary gunfight ever fought in the American West. During the shooting Tom and Frank McClaury and Billy Clanton were killed and several others wounded, including Doc Holliday. Both Doc Holliday and Wyatt were arrested for murder but quickly released and cleared of the charges.

Life in Tombstone just seemed to get worse and repercussions from the fight led to Morgan Earp being ambushed and killed, and Virgil attacked and injured. This set brother Wyatt off on the Earp Vendetta Ride, in which Doc Holliday accompanied Wyatt.

Wyatt was appointed as Deputy US Marshall after Virgil's injuries left him unable to continue his role. Wyatt then deputised Warren Earp, James Earp, Sherman McMaster, Doc Holliday and 'Turkey Creek' Jack Johnson.

Virgil needed to recoup from his injuries and it was decided that going back home would help his recovery. Guarded by Wyatt and his deputies, he left with his family by train for Colton, California. Morgan's coffin was on board the train for a burial in Colton.

Wyatt's deputies acted as protection for Virgil on the journey but on arrival in Tucson in 1882, Ike Clanton and Frank Stilwell were spotted at the station hiding, and it was suspected that they were there to finish off Virgil. Frank Stilwell was soon found riddled with bullets not long after the sighting.

Wyatt's deputies continue the hunt for more suspects in Morgan's killing and Florentino "Indian Charlie" Cruz became their latest victim.

Wyatt and Holliday parted company not long after this although it seems to have been over an argument over a woman, but on many occasions

Wyatt came to Holliday's rescue. One particular time Doc Holliday was accused of the murder of Frank Stilwell and arrested in Arizona. Wyatt was able to prove otherwise and Doc Holliday was released.

By now Holliday was a very sick man. But this did not stop many trying to 'best' him in the gunfighter stakes. Luckily for Holliday, his very light weight due to his illness, stood him in good stead as in 1885 when he claimed self-defence as he 'feared for his life' when William J. 'Billy' Allen was shot in the arm by Holliday. Holliday owed him money and Allen wanted it back. Holliday was concerned that there could be trouble over this debt and spoke to Marshall Harvey Faucet about the situation. Faucett told Holliday that Allen did not carry a weapon and Holliday is said to have said, "I'll get a shotgun and shoot him on sight".

Faucett tried to warn Allen of this but failed to find him in time. And on entering Hyman's Saloon, Holliday aimed and missed the first time, then shot him in the arm severing a main artery. He lived and was patched up but his arm didn't work quite right afterwards apparently.

Holliday was arrested and put on trial and it seems like a technicality in the law of the day called 'No Duty to Retreat' helped get Holliday acquitted. 'No Duty to Retreat' was a *'belief, enacted in the laws of several states, that a man who was without blame for provoking a confrontation was not obliged to flee from his assailant but was free to stand his ground regardless of the consequences.'* Wikipedia

This allowed for Holliday to be acquitted of any crime.

After meeting Wyatt in various locations just to avoid any further troubles, they eventually meet up in Glenwood Springs, Colorado. Doc Holliday's health continued to deteriorate and by now he was very dependent on alcohol and laudanum to try and ease his symptoms of tuberculosis. His condition affected his ability to gamble and the coughing fits were very severe.

Public Domain Image

In the Hotel Glenwood, Glenwood Springs, Colorado, Doc Holliday had hoped that the hot springs there would alleviate some of the symptoms. But on 8th November, 1887 Doc Holliday died of the disease. The sulphurous fumes may have done more harm than good.

Holliday had apparently always thought that he would die with his boots on. But at 10.00 am on 8th November, 1887 his last words are said to have been, "This is funny", as he looked down on his bootless feet while he drank his last whiskey. He was only 36 years old.

Wyatt Earp in 1896 said of Holliday, *"I found him a loyal friend and good company. He was a dentist whom necessity had made a gambler; a gentleman whom disease had made a vagabond; a philosopher whom life had made a caustic wit; a long, lean blonde fellow nearly dead with consumption and at the same time the most skilful gambler and nerviest, speediest, deadliest man with a six-gun I ever knew."* Wikipedia

BUFFALO BILL CODY

After a peaceful spell in Canada, hunger and desperation led Sitting Bull to surrender himself and his people on 19th July, 1881 at Fort Buford. Shortly after this he and his people were held as prisoners of war in Fort Randall, South Dakota, and it wasn't until 1883 that he led his people to Fort Yates at the Standing Rock Agency where they made their lives.

Sitting Bull was classed as a bit of a trouble maker, so when a suggestion came from Buffalo Bill Cody that Sitting Bull became part of his Wild West Show, the Indian Agent, James McLaughlin, jumped at the chance to be rid of him for a time. If he wasn't on the reservation, then he couldn't start any uprisings.

Imagine how exciting it must have been for all those ticket holders to watch the spectacle of Buffalo Bill's Wild West Show. To be there, and to watch those 'savages' getting their comeuppance at last. Even if it was all pretence.

And the whole idea proved very lucrative for Buffalo Bill Cody.

But Buffalo Bill Cody was much more than this. And he started his career very early on as, when aged 11, he took a role as a 'boy extra' riding up and down between the length of the wagon train to deliver messages to drivers and workmen.

He also earned the name of 'Indian fighter' when he shot and killed a Sioux warrior who was aiming his arrow at a colleague of Cody's.

But, like many others, gold fever caught Cody at the age of 14 years and he headed off to make his fortune. But instead, on his way to the California Gold Rush, he met and signed up for the Pony Express as a rider. Whether this story is true or not, it does make his life very good reading, as Cody was extremely good at publicising himself and may have fabricated some of his roles during his lifetime.

But it could be that he was the Pony Express rider who made the longest nonstop ride from Red Buttes Station to Rocky Ridge Station and back when he discovered his relief rider had been killed. This was a total of

322 miles in 21 hours and 40 minutes using 21 horses to complete the ride. Sounds quite a feat. Or it could just be a really interesting story.

Public Domain Image

Public Domain Image
Buffalo Bill

But he did serve as a private in Company H, 7th Kansas Cavalry, in the Union Army from 1863 – 1865. This much we do know. Plus he got married in 1866 and produced four children, two who sadly died young. And 1866 saw him re-united with his old friend Wild Bill Hickok who was acting as a scout for the US Army. Cody signed up too and worked with George Custer for a spell.

Public Domain Image

During 1867 he was given a leave of absence so that he could help supply the railway workers of the Kansas Pacific Railway with buffalo meat. His reputation as a buffalo hunter came from this part of his life, as Cody is said to have killed 4,282 buffalo in eighteen months between 1867-1868. And it gave him the name of Buffalo Bill Cody.

His reputation had to be proved though as he was challenged by another buffalo hunter, Bill Comstock, and they had an eight hour buffalo shooting match. He proved that the name of Buffalo Bill Cody was apt and deserved when he killed 68 buffalo to Comstock's 48.

Public Domain Image

Public Domain Image

185

After his very successfully spell of a year, he then returned to active service in 1868 as a despatch rider covering a total of 350 miles in 58 hours through very hostile territory apparently walking the last 35 miles.

He was rewarded with the role of Chief of Scouts for the 5th Cavalry Regiment and was also performed this role for the 3rd Cavalry later.

His efforts as Chief of Scouts didn't go un-noticed and in 1872 he was awarded the Medal of Honour for gallantry. Sadly this medal was revoked in 1917 along with many others who had received it, when the War Department changed the regulations for awarding this 'highest military honour', but long after his death his family were able to gain restoration of the medal for himself and other civilian scouts.

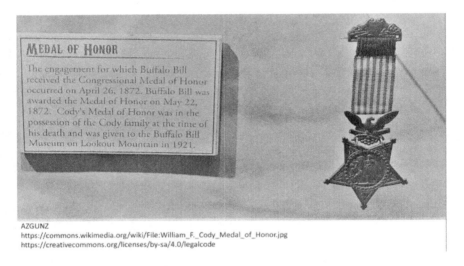

MEDAL OF HONOR

The engagement for which Buffalo Bill received the Congressional Medal of Honor occurred on April 26, 1872. Buffalo Bill was awarded the Medal of Honor on May 22, 1872. Cody's Medal of Honor was in the possession of the Cody family at the time of his death and was given to the Buffalo Bill Museum on Lookout Mountain in 1921.

AZGUNZ
https://commons.wikimedia.org/wiki/File:William_F._Cody_Medal_of_Honor.jpg
https://creativecommons.org/licenses/by-sa/4.0/legalcode

But I think what he is better remembered for are the Wild West Shows.

They were basically travelling vaudeville shows starting around the 1870s up until the whole idea waned in the 1920s and they sensationalised the whole concept of the Wild West. But they were loved by many and extremely popular.

And it all started when a man called Ned Buntline wrote a novel about one particular hero in 1869, a buffalo hunter, US Army scout and also a guide. The novel was called ***Buffalo Bill, the King of Border Men***. Cody was in print and this added to his fame. Buntline had met Buffalo Bill on a train and was fascinated by his life, hence the novel. And Buffalo Bill's notoriety began.

Public Domain Image

In December 1872, Cody travelled to Chicago to act in the show 'The Scouts of the Prairie' with his friend Texas Jack Omohundro. Wild Bill Hickok was asked along to join the show but he didn't take to the 'grease paint' and the acting life at all and left after a few months.

The storyline and even some of the characters did, or had, existed, but the Native American was always portrayed as the 'bad guy'. And got many a hefty 'booooo' from the crowds for their trouble.

Buffalo Bill's Wild West Show was a huge success wherever it went. So successful that it toured Europe eight times between 1887 and 1892 with the last tours happening in 1902 to 1906. The first tour became part of the American Exhibition with the Golden Jubilee of Queen Victoria.

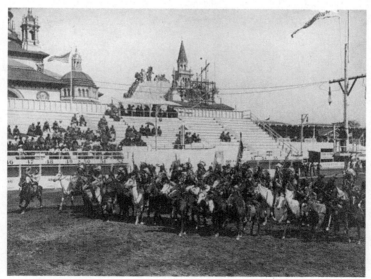

Public Domain Image

The shows were lengthy affairs lasting about 3-4 hours. But with marvellous displays of sharpshooting, hunts, races, rodeo events, they were worth the long sit down for the thousands that attended.

In 1893 he changed the name of the show to *'Buffalo Bill's Wild West and Congress of Rough Riders of the World'*. After a parade on horseback to start the show, massive battle re-enactments would be the norm, with a buffalo hunt, a train robbery, Pony Express riders and of course those pesky 'Indians' attacking wagon trains, stage coaches and making war on the white man. The most famous being in the shape of *'Custer's Last Stand'*. What a sight that must have been for the audience. And this is where Sitting Bull and a band of his braves performed. And who saved the day? Why, the lone figure of Buffalo Bill of course riding into the melee and shooting those 'savages'. For effect only I hasten to add.

Not only did the Native Americans entertain the crowd with their staged battles, but they were told to act out "savagery and wildness" against the white settlers also in the show. This depicted the Native American as cruel savage beasts that the white man already felt that they were.

They might have been thought of by the public as 'savage beast' but Buffalo Bill 'respected and supported' them. *"He offered 'good pay and a change to improve their lives'. He described them as 'former foe, present friend, the American' and once said that 'every Indian outbreak that I have known has resulted from broken promises and broken treaties by the government.' "* Wikipedia

'Many of them took along their family members and were encouraged to 'set up camp just as they would in their homelands'. He wanted the paying public to see the human side of the 'fierce warriors'. Wikipedia

Public Domain Image

Sitting Bull joined the show 1884, and stayed with the show for four months before returning home. During that time, audiences considered him a celebrity and thought of him as an exceptional warrior, which he was. He earned a small fortune by charging for his autograph and his picture, so he had a business head on his shoulders. Then he often gave his money away to the homeless and beggars of the US he found living on the streets.

But the finale of the show must have been a sight to see as it was usually based on an Indian attack on a white settler's burning cabin, with the Indians being seen off by Buffalo Bill and his cowboys.

Public Domain Image

All good family stuff. And it didn't stop there. There were shooting competitions and skill was shown in the many displays of marksmanship. Annie Oakley being a major part of this, with her talent with guns and rifles. As was Calamity Jane who was famous as a notorious frontierswoman and the subject of many wild stories, many she made up herself, but they probably made better stories that way. In the show, she was a skilled horsewoman and expert rifle and revolver handler. But sadly this ended in 1902, when she was reportedly sacked from the show for drinking and fighting.

Public Domain Image

Public Domain Image
Annie Oakley

Buffalo Bill's Wild West Shows travelled the world and proved to be very popular. He became an international celebrity.

Public Domain Image

But by the 1900s people could go and see the Wild West at its best at any local cinema. Silent movies, yes, but there was no travelling to where Buffalo Bill's Show was held. This led to the demise of his shows even though he tried to continue, but the cinema competition was too great.

By 1908 the Buffalo Bill and Pawnee Bill Film Company had been formed in New York City which produced a three reel film called '*The Life of Buffalo Bill*'. Cody was the star and it's now part of history in the Library of Congress. The Two Bills Show also in 1908 where the two Wild West legends joined forces to create a show, was not a success and failed.

His health deteriorating, Buffalo Bill died on 10th January, 1917, of kidney failure. He received tributes from very influential people that he had met. King George V, Kaiser Wilhelm II, and President Woodrow Wilson, and many attended his funeral on 3rd June,1917.

Public Domain Image

His show was sold that month for $105,000 (about $2,121,000 today).

Public Domain Image

BUTCH CASSIDY AND THE SUNDANCE KID, THE WILD BUNCH AND THE HOLE IN THE WALL HIDEOUT

A bit further down the era, a famous gang appeared. The Hole in the Wall gang which many of you will have heard of thanks to programmes like 'Alias Smith and Jones', two gang members (Kid Curry and Hannibal Hayes) who wanted to seek amnesty and tried to stay out of trouble. But in truth, the Hole in the Wall gang wasn't just one gang. It was made up of several gangs operating out of the same base at Hole in the Wall Pass with some well-known gang members.

Famous names like Harry Alonzo Longabaugh, better known as the Sundance Kid, and Robert LeRoy Parker, better known as Butch Cassidy, used the Hole in the Wall Pass as their hideout. Both men were known for bank robbery, train robbery, outlaws, thieves and gang leaders.

Parker came from a Mormon family but left home as a teenager and started working on a dairy farm before meeting cattle thief Mike Cassidy.

JERRYE AND ROY KLOTZ MD
https://commons.wikimedia.org/wiki/File:MAHR_BUILDING,_TELLURIDE,_COLORADO.jpg
MAHR BUILDING
TELLURIDE, COLORADO https://creativecommons.org/licenses/by-sa/3.0/legalcode

Parker's first claim to fame however was rather a minor one. In 1879 he discovered the shop he intended to visit was closed so he broke in. He stole a pair of jeans and some pie but he did leave an IOU promising to pay the next time he visited. The shop pressed charges but Parker was acquitted by a jury.

After a move to Frisco, Utah, with his parents, Parker started work on the Jim Marshall Ranch nearby and this is when he met a man called Mike Cassidy, and because of their friendship, this inspired Parker to change his name to Cassidy. Mike Cassidy changed Parker/Cassidy's life dramatically when he initiated him into the huge world beyond where his, and other Mormon families, lived. Mike Cassidy gave him a gun and showed him how to use it. By 1887 Parker/Cassidy, while being totally fascinated by the saloons and gambling halls in Telluride, found a role packing ore and made money to help him in his new hobby. On the gambling tables.

He also met a man called Matt Warner, a racehorse owner, and they raced a horse at various events and made money to share between them. These winnings and the quest for more easy money, led to Cassidy's first bank robbery in 1889 at the San Miguel Valley Bank in Telluride with two of the McCarty brothers, stealing $21,000 (about $605,000). They then fled to Robbers Roost in Utah.

Public Domain Image

A brief time as an apprentice butcher in Rock Springs, Wyoming, his nickname changed to Butch. Because of his friendship with Cassidy, Parker permanently changed his surname to Cassidy. And Butch Cassidy was born.

In 1890 Cassidy bought a ranch near to the location of the Hole in the Wall hideout, possibly as a pretence to hide his activities in crime. Even if it was, Cassidy still had his own brand for his cattle.

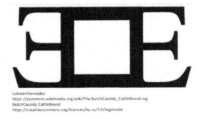
Lobsterthermidor
https://commons.wikimedia.org/wiki/File:ButchCassidy_CattleBrand.svg
ButchCassidy CattleBrand
https://creativecommons.org/licenses/by-sa/3.0/legalcode

In 1894 Cassidy became involved with outlaw Ann Bassett, whose father Cassidy knew and did business with through cattle and horse supplies.

But this year also saw his arrest for horse stealing and his imprisonment in Wyoming State Penitentiary in Laramie. He was imprisoned for 18 months.

After a brief involvement with Bassett's older sister Josie, Cassidy returned to his former love Ann.

But this saw the start of Cassidy's association with a very large circle of criminals from that time who became known as 'The Wild Bunch'.

The Wild Bunch consisted of friend William Ellsworth "Elzy" Lay, Harvey "Kid Curry" Logan, Ben Kilpatrick, Harry Tracy, Will "News" Carver, Laura Bullion and George "Flat Nose" Curry. In 1896, Cassidy came across Harry Alonzo Longabaugh (Sundance Kid) after Cassidy, Lay and Logan had robbed the bank in Montpelier, Idaho.

Public Domain Image

Public Domain Image

Front row left to right: Harry Alonzo Longabaugh, alias the Sundance Kid, Ben Kilpatrick, alias the Tall Texan, Robert Leroy Parker, alias Butch Cassidy

Standing: Will Carver, alias News Carver, & Harvey Logan, alias Kid Curry; Fort Worth, Texas, 1900

THIS PHOTO WAS USED BY THE PINKERTON AGENCY ON WANTED POSTERS

Public Domain Image

Harry Alonzo Longabaugh, better known as the Sundance Kid, was born in 1867, had originally had a normal start in life by finding work as a wrangler on a neighbour's ranch in Colorado, and learning the skill of buying and breeding horses.

1886 saw Longabaugh working on various ranches until 1887. Then his life seemed to take a u-tune as he stole a gun, horse and saddle from a ranch in Sundance, Wyoming. He was caught and sentenced to 18 months in jail and it was here that he adopted the name he will be remembered for, the Sundance Kid.

After his release he worked on various ranches ending up in Alberta, Canada on the Bar U Ranch in 1891 and he even became a joint owner of a saloon in the Grand Central Hotel, Calgary. But this didn't last long before he was rustling cattle and horses in Montana and Canada while working with the N Bar N Ranch.

Sundance was suspected of being part of a train robbery in 1892 with Bill Madden and Harry Bass. The latter two are caught and sentenced to prison. Sundance escaped.

Sometime afterwards, and keeping himself out of the lime light, the Sundance Kid built a great reputation as a horse wrangler, using Harry Alonzo as his new name. This was 1895-1896 but soon the Sundance Kid is back robbing a bank in South Dakota.

He was now part of the Wild Bunch and as he was very fast with the gun, and he would have been a bonus to the gang. But it is said that he did not kill anyone, despite being very quick on the draw. But he was now closely associated with Cassidy and the Wild Bunch.

Robbers Roost was the place of safety for the Wild Bunch to plan their next and many other robberies. In one robbery they stole $7,000 from the payroll of the Pleasant Mining Valley Coal Company in 1897, followed by a robbery to the Union Pacific Overland Flyer passenger train in 1899 stealing between $30,000 - $50,000.

Charlie Siringo

And this drew them to the attention of the Pinkerton National Detective Agency. Charlie Siringo was assigned to capture the outlaws.

One robbery, which Cassidy may have planned, led to the death of Sheriff Edward Farr killed by William Lay, one of the Wild Bunch. Lay was convicted of the murder and sentenced to life imprisonment in the New Mexico State Penitentiary. This led to the Wild Bunch heading in different directions for safety. Cassidy had a different idea.

It is said that he approached Utah Governor Heber Wells in the hope of amnesty. Well's advice was to ask the Union Pacific Railroad to drop all criminal complaints against him. But it is said that he was also warned that he had many criminal charges against him and that he would always be a wanted man. After this information, it seemed pointless to meet up with the Union Pacific Chairman E. H. Harriman. Cassidy and Sundance and some of the other gang members robbed a Union Pacific train instead.

Sundance Kid and Etta Place

But things were starting to get quite tough, as many of the original Wild Bunch were now being arrested or killed and the Pinkertons were in pursuit. There was only one thing to do. Cassidy and the Sundance Kid fled the area to New York City with the Sundance Kid's companion, Etta Place. But even then they knew they were not safe from the continuous pursuit of the law and moved themselves to Buenos Aires, Argentina, on the British steamer SS Herminius in February, 1901. They bought a ranch and settled down near Rio Blanco near Cholila east of the Andes. For a time.

But strangely enough, two English speaking bandits held up the Banco de Tarapaca y Argentino in February, 1905. But Butch Cassidy and the Sundance Kid were said to be somewhere else at the time. This robbery alerted the Pinkertons of their locality and again Cassidy, Sundance and Place were on the move again. Robbing different banks on the way.

But historians say that Place had had enough of life on the run and returned to the US. Some say that she was involved with one particular bank robbery in Villa Mercedes, was injured and possibly died of her injuries. Again history is vague here.

In the meantime, Cassidy found himself a role, as a guard, in the Concordia Tin Mine in the Santa Vera Cruz in Bolivia. He used the name of James 'Santiago' Maxwell and sometimes George Lowe while Sundance was Frank Smith. They were working at the camp of a gold dredging operation near Esmoraca, Bolivia, at the time.

By 1908 the payroll carrier of the Cia Solver Mine was attacked and robbed by two Americans thought to be Cassidy and Sundance. They were spotted a few days later in San Vincente staying in a boarding house and suspicions were aroused.

What happens next is open for debate. I am writing the information I have found regarding their demise but history is undecided as to what really happened. They may not have been in the area at the time, as some say that Butch Cassidy was in Alaska and the Sundance Kid was in San Francisco. So don't take it as read just in-case.

Alerted to their whereabouts, on 7th November, 1908, the local cavalry regiment, surround the boarding house and the shooting soon started lasting several hours into the night. Cries were heard from inside the boarding house with two shots fired in succession. Then all was silent.

The next morning the boarding house was entered and the bodies of two men were found riddled with bullets. One assumed to be Sundance had a bullet wound to the forehead, while the other man had a bullet hole in his temple. They speculated that the positioning of the bodies meant that Sundance had been fatally wounded and in order to put him out of his misery, Cassidy had shot him before shooting himself. The Bolivian authorities, even though they said that these were the bodies of the payroll robbers, didn't know their names, nor could they positively identify them either. The bodies were buried at the San Vincente cemetery and although their graves have been sought after and bones have been found, no positive DNA has been found to prove that it was Butch Cassidy and the Sundance Kid.

It has been speculated that both men survived and returned to the United States, and that Sundance lived in Utah under the name of William Henry Long. Long died in 1936 and his remains were exhumed in 2008 for DNA testing but his remains did not match any relatives DNA.

Josie Bassett, Cassidy's girlfriend, stated that she had a visit from Cassidy in the 1920s and that he died about 1945. And others have made similar claims over the years.

Whatever happened, their legend will live on and the speculation as to what really happened just makes it all the more fascinating.

THEN AND NOW

Public Domain Image

Public Domain Image

THEN AND NOW

But times were now changing. The Wild West was not as wild as it had been. People were settling in cities that had once been boomtowns and the life of a cowboy, gunslinger or card sharp was declining rapidly.

But legends have been born and are still the topic of many programmes, books and films. And long may it continue.

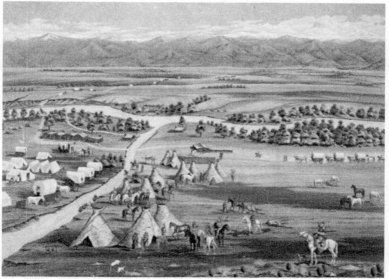

Public Domain Image

Boomtown Denver 1859

Public Domain Image

Denver 1898

Flickr user: Larry Johnson https://www.flickr.com/people/drljohnson/
https://commons.wikimedia.org/wiki/File:Denver_skyline.jpg
Denver skyline
https://creativecommons.org/licenses/by/2.0/legalcode

Denver now

Public Domain Image

Boomtown San Francisco 1850

Public Domain Image

San Francisco 1878

Noah Friedlander
https://commons.wikimedia.org/wiki/File:San_Francisco_from_the_Marin_Headlands_in_March_2019.jpg
https://creativecommons.org/licenses/by-sa/4.0/legalcode

San Francisco now

Public Domain Image

Boomtown Tombstone 1881

Grombo
https://commons.wikimedia.org/wiki/File:Allen_Street_Tombstone.jpg
Allen Street Tombstone
https://creativecommons.org/licenses/by-sa/3.0/legalcode

Tombstone 2021

Boomtown Deadwood 1876

Deadwood 2021

POST SCRIPT

The expansion was over. America's Manifest Destiny had originally required a specific amount of land that needed to be conquered. Now it had.

Those brave pioneering settlers, definitely a hardy bunch of people, coming from just about everywhere, had pushed west to get a better life for themselves and their families. A new life.

Some new settlers had heard about this wonderful land from relatives who had already succeeded in settling in the west, inspiring others to follow. And who can blame them?

It was a huge opportunity offering a **promise of independence and prosperity to anyone willing to** meet the hardships of frontier life.

The land was cheap and there was lots of it with good soil for farming. This was a motivator for a lot of settlers. Land was a symbol of wealth in Europe and about five million people came to the United States. Land was unavailable on the East Coast, so the west was the place to be.

Theodore Roosevelt said of female settlers, *"There is an old border saying that frontier is hard on women and cattle. A rule that the grinding toil of hardship and the vast wilderness drives the beauty of a woman long before her youth has left her. By the time she is a mother she is angular compressed lips, sallow brow, but there is a hundred qualities that atone for the grace she lacks. Clad in a dingy gown and a hideous sun bonnet she goes gaily about her work."*

But there was also the opportunity to get rich quick with the gold and silver mining and the logging. And if you had a mind to it, earning your living as a card sharp gaining the gold and silver through gambling. An easy life? Only if you were good with a gun when it all fell foul and their opponents didn't like losing their gold or silver to a cardsharp.

The expansion continued and America grew with farmers being successful and housing being built. Towns sprang up and still remain and the populace thrived. But at what expense?

206

This expansion had a huge impact on the Native American. Sadly it was the Native American who lost all this land to the 'white man'. They not only lost their lands, their way of life, but they also lost a food source. The buffalo. This led to many a conflict between the white man and the Native American as we now know leading to many deaths on both sides. But the Native American still ended up on very small reservations, very unhappily I must add.

And this westward expansion made America a superpower.

But historians do say that the west was 'wild' with parts of it being more dangerous than others. Most likely in those places where gold and other minerals were discovered. Fighting for your rights here, committing murder to protect your home or your stake and physical assault were not uncommon during these 'wild' times.

But like everything else these things do come to an end and again historians say that the 'wild west' ended around 1900. But out of some of those boomtowns, those trading posts, turned into cities like Los Angeles, San Francisco, Denver, New York and Seattle and many others are now some of the greatest cities of the world. Growing, ever growing, with people moulding their own destinies.

And America is still the 'land of opportunity'. People still flock there to make their fortune or become famous. They still endure hardships while they try to establish themselves in this 'land of the free'. Until that great day, when they make their mark and their lives change for the better. Many have gone there and failed, but many have succeeded.

The land itself is built on the determination of those pioneers from way back fighting to survive and make a living on the land. Those pioneers may be long gone now, but the land they toiled on, fought and died on has now been handed down from generation to generation. And their courage and determination must have inspired their children and their children's children. All part and parcel of the American Dream.

The 'American Dream' is was a term given by James Truslow Adams in 1931 saying that "life should be better and richer and fuller for everyone, with opportunity for each according to ability or achievement" regardless of social class or circumstances of birth achieved by hard work.

It's also part of the Declaration of Independence, which proclaims that *"all men are created equal"* with the right to *"life, liberty, and the*

207

pursuit of happiness." Also, the US Constitution promotes similar freedom, in the Preamble to ***"secure the Blessings of Liberty to ourselves and our Posterity"***. Wikipedia

Marvellous words and words that seal many decisions to head to America and attain that *'better life'*. No matter where you are from or what you do, America could be right for you.

It sounds like an advert for moving there and it probably is and many will go there. Continuing the American Dream and making it theirs and building further on the expansion that started all those years ago.

Many have come and gone in that vast timescale but they have left their mark giving America its fascinating history and very memorable names and lives to remember and in some cases admire their tenacity for success.

I hope that you, the reader, have learnt and enjoyed reading about the ***Days of the Old Wild West*** in America. Even though this book is just a fraction of the vast history that made America what it is today. Those Wild West days that still entertain us in films and books and will do so for many a year to come. About those brave, enterprising people, who played their part, opening up that vast frontier, who actually made the history of America.

Yippee ki yay

BIBLIOGRAPHY

BOOKS USED FOR REFERENCE

- ✪ The American West by Royal B Hassrick
- ✪ The Icons of the Wild West by Charles River Editors
- ✪ Legends of the Wild West by Robert Edelstein
- ✪ Outlaws of the Wild West by Terry C Treadwell
- ✪ The Wild West – History, Myth and the Making of America by Frederick Nolan
- ✪ Comanche Life by Carol Dean
- ✪ A Man Called Sitting Bull by Carol Dean
- ✪ Geronimo and Cochise – Two Apache Legends by Carol Dean
- ✪ Quanah Parker – One Man - Two Worlds by Carol Dean
- ✪ Joseph G. Rosa's book They called him Wild Bill, the life and adventures of James Butler Hickok

WEBSITES USED AS REFERENCE

- ✪ https://en.wikipedia.org/wiki/Battle_of_the_Alamo
- ✪ https://en.wikipedia.org/wiki/Billy_the_Kid
- ✪ https://en.wikipedia.org/wiki/Black_Hills_Gold_Rush
- ✪ https://en.wikipedia.org/wiki/Bozeman_Trail
- ✪ https://en.wikipedia.org/wiki/Buffalo_Bill
- ✪ https://www.legendsofamerica.com/we-buffalohunters
- ✪ https://en.wikipedia.org/wiki/Butch_Cassidy
- ✪ https://en.wikipedia.org/wiki/Butterfield_Overland_Mail
- ✪ https://en.wikipedia.org/wiki/Davy_Crockett
- ✪ https://en.wikipedia.org/wiki/Daniel_Boone
- ✪ https://en.wikipedia.org/wiki/Doc_Holliday
- ✪ https://en.wikipedia.org/wiki/Frank_James
- ✪ https://en.wikipedia.org/wiki/Jesse_James
- ✪ https://en.wikipedia.org/wiki/Jim_Bridger
- ✪ https://en.wikipedia.org/wiki/John_Wesley_Hardin
- ✪ https://en.wikipedia.org/wiki/Harvey_Logan

- https://en.wikipedia.org/wiki/Pat_Garret
- https://en.wikipedia.org/wiki/Pike%27s_Peak_Gold_Rush
- https://en.wikipedia.org/wiki/Pony_Express
- https://en.wikipedia.org/wiki/Santa_Fe_Trail
- https://en.wikipedia.org/wiki/Sundance_Kid
- https://en.wikipedia.org/wiki/Oregon_Trail
  https://en.wikipedia.org/wiki/Wells_Fargo_(1852%E2%80%931998)
- https://en.wikipedia.org/wiki/Wild_Bill_Hickok
- https://en.wikipedia.org/wiki/Wild_West_shows
- https://en.wikipedia.org/wiki/Transcontinental_railroad
- https://en.wikipedia.org/wiki/Texas_annexation
- https://en.wikipedia.org/wiki/San_Francisco
- https://en.wikipedia.org/wiki/Columbia,_California
- https://en.wikipedia.org/wiki/Cattle_drives_in_the_United_States
- https://en.wikipedia.org/wiki/Sitting_Bull#Surrender
- https://en.wikipedia.org/wiki/Bushwhacker#Jesse_James
- https://en.wikipedia.org/wiki/Robert_Ford_(outlaw)#Killing_Jesse_James
- https://en.wikipedia.org/wiki/James%E2%80%93Younger_Gang#Northfield,_Minnesota_Raid
- https://en.wikipedia.org/wiki/American_Dream
- https://en.wikipedia.org/wiki/Black_Hills_Expedition
- https://en.wikipedia.org/wiki/American_frontier#Law_and_order
- https://en.wikipedia.org/wiki/California_Gold_Rush
- http://timelinesandsoundtracks.blogspot.com/2019/02/doc-holliday-timeline.html
- https://www.pbs.org/wgbh/americanexperience/features/wyatt-earp-life
- http://www.aboutbillythekid.com/chronology.htm
- https://worldhistoryproject.org/topics/buffalo-bill
- https://murderpedia.org/male.H/h/hardin-john-wesley.htm
- http://timelinesandsoundtracks.blogspot.com/2020/11/butch-cassidy-timeline.html
- http://timelinesandsoundtracks.blogspot.com/2020/11/sundance-kid-timeline.html
- http://timelinesandsoundtracks.blogspot.com/2018/10/pat-garrett-timeline.html
- https://www.legendsofamerica.com/we-jessejamestimeline
- https://worldhistoryproject.org/topics/james-butler-wild-bill-hickok
- https://en.wikipedia.org/wiki/Fence_Cutting_Wars
- https://en.wikipedia.org/wiki/Warren_Earp

DVDs USED FOR REFERENCE

✪ The Alamo starring John Wayne
✪ Open Range documentary narrated by Kevin Costner

IMAGES USED

Used Through the book

© Image by Alexander Lesnitsky from Pixabay

Used on cover

© Image by Calmer-Free-Vector-Images from Pixabay

Louisiana Purchase – Page 5

Rocky Mountains – Page 11

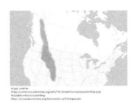

Yellowstone Grand Geyser – Page 12

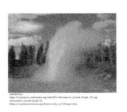

Green River Map – Page 14

Bozeman Trail – Page 15, 89

Jim Bridger – Page 16

The Oregon Trail – Page 18

Oklahoma Indian Territories – Page 32, 83

The Alamo – Page 33

The Alamo Memorial – Page 38

Californian Gold Fields – Page 41

South Platte Basin – Page 46

Wells Fargo Bank – Page 51

Butterfield Overland Mail Service – Page 52

Red Caboose Lantern – Page 60

Sand Creek Massacre – Page 86

Pat Garratt's Grave Stone – Page 133

Deadwood – Page 156, 205

Dead Man's Hand - Page 157

Wild Bill Hickok Momument at Deadwood – Page 157

Buffalo Bill's Medal – Page 186

Telluride – Page 193

Butch Cassidy's Cattle Brand – Page 194

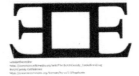

Robbers Roost – Page 197

Denver as it is now – Page 202

San Francisco as it is now – Page 203

Tombstone as it is now – Page 204

INDEX

ALSO AVAILABLE BY CAROL DEAN

The Comanche were the fiercest and most feared of tribes. A warring tribe.

And a tribe, a people, fighting to preserve their traditions, values and the land they loved.

Find out how such a tribe lived their everyday lives, and how the Comanche almost fell into obscurity with the help of the 'white man', and how they rose again to be the Comanche Nation that they are today.

Available in hardback or paperback – black and white or colour.

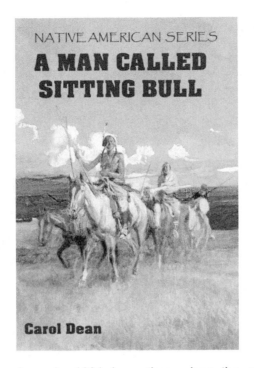

Sitting Bull was born in 1831 in a time when the white man had descended on the Sioux tribal lands and claimed it for themselves. A turbulent time that continued throughout his life. A life of devotion to his family, caring for his tribe, courageous and brave in the face of danger and a gifted communicator with the animals and the Great Spirit.

His tribe held him in high esteem and spoke of his 'big medicine' which was a huge compliment to the man.

And that's only a small part of the man himself. Learn about the legend that was and is Chief Sitting Bull and perhaps you too will admire the man he became.

Available in hardback or paperback – black and white or colour.

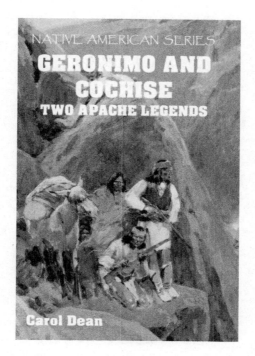

Over the years the Apache have been led by many legendary people. Two well known Apache legends, and the two that I have chosen to write about, are Geronimo and Cochise.

They lived in turbulent times. Times when these two legends needed to join forces to fight for their lands and the lives of their people against the Mexican and the American soldiers. Both forces seeking revenge and retribution for the deaths of loved ones at the hands of the white man's army, and the loss of their sacred lands desecrated by the white man.

Geronimo and Cochise's joint forces became a daring, dynamic and powerful fighting force to be reckoned with and feared.

This is their story.

Available in hardback or paperback – black and white or colour

Carol Dean's book takes you back to the days of the Comanche and their struggle against the white man. Quanah Parker became one man living in two worlds as he was the last chief the Comanche ever had.

This book takes the reader through Parker's assimilation into the white man's world and the great success he made of it and describes how he became a major part of American history and still is today.

Carol's book "Comanche Life" contains a brief summary of Quanah's life as he was the last chief of the Comanche. This book provides a fuller picture of this incredible man.

In the year 1830 President Andrew Jackson signed and had approved the Indian Removal Act. For the Five Civilised Tribes of Native America, the Choctaw, Chickasaw, Seminole, Muscagee (Creek), and the Cherokee, this meant the end of their lives as they knew it and the start of the Trail of Tears.

A trail that, not only brought tears, but has become famous for the starvation, disease, despair and death amongst the Five Civilised Tribes that were forced to travel on it.

An unbelievably sad story, said to be the most sorrowful legacy of the Jacksonian Era.

But it's all true.

The Native American has for many hundreds of years fought long and hard through many battles and suffered broken treaties to try to hold onto their lands and traditions. Many famous Native Americans have been noted and credited for the successes, or failures, of some of those well known battles. Names that we all know and recognise, and will live on in history forever.

But there are others, perhaps not so famous, who played their part in the Native American history. This book mentions just some of them. A few that I personally have chosen to honour, through this book, for their part. And there are many, many more.

Read how history was shaped as *They Too Played Their Part*.

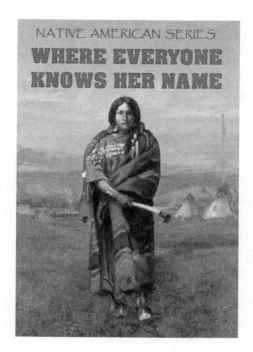

Many famous battles throughout Native American and American history have been fought with both sides gaining victories or incurring losses. But those battles were fought by many famous warriors of the time. And not all of them were male warriors.

This book entitled, 'Where Everyone Knows Her Name' delves into the lives and the bravery of some of the female warriors fighting alongside their male compatriots and winning through in those battles.

Some names you will recognise, and some will be new to you. But put them altogether and read about the courage, determination, and valour these female warriors showed in the face of danger. This book covers only a few of these impressive and powerful women in history. Women that I have personally chosen to write about. It's to remember those women and all the others in history too. And there are so many more.

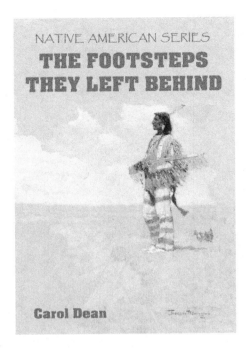

When reading about Native Americans, not many will consider exactly what Native Americans are doing now. That's understandable considering the appalling history of battles for lands, traditions, and their cultures under the white man's hands. No set of peoples or civilisations have ever had to face such trauma as the Native Americans have for hundreds of years. That's the history that is read about, understood, and hopefully learnt from so that it never happens again.

But Native Americans have come through everything that they have had thrown at them over the years, and are now making a new history. A history of renewed interest and learning in their cultures, language, traditions, and their turbulent past. With many Native Americans reaching great heights in a very competitive world.

This book covers that new Native American history and honours just some of those involved.